Better Homes Cookery

CAKES and BAKING

Myra Street

COLLINS LONDON AND GLASGOW

Cover Photograph by courtesy of the Australian Recipe Service.
Photography by Roy Rich, Angel Studios.

Copyright © Meredith Corporation, 1971
Printed in Great Britain by Collins of Glasgow and London

ISBN 0 00 435514 8

Acknowledgements

	Pages	
Flour Advisory Bureau	8–9	Bread Making
	11	Enriched Bread
	11	Wheatmeal Bread
	13	Croissants
	15	Bara Brith
	44	Simnel Cake
	49	Swiss Roll
	72	Mince Pies
J. W. French & Co Ltd	20	Chelsea Buns
Fruit Producers Council	47	Gingerbread
	60	Pastry
Kraft	25	Scotch Pancakes
	72	Cornish Pasties
	76	Flaky Pastry
	78	Puff Pastry
McDougall's Cookery Service	11	Pizza
	28	Raisin Bread
	34	Scones
	37	Victoria Sandwich Cake
	38	Sponge Flan
	42	Fruit Cake
	45	Gingerbread
	48	Whisked Sponge
	70	Pastry Boats

Contents

Baking is not an art but a craft that anyone can learn. Yet there are many who would have us believe that successful bakers are endowed with magical gifts that are denied to lesser mortals. I'll let you into the secret. Successful baking can be mastered by anyone who is prepared to follow simple instructions . . . *to the letter.*

But why bother to bake in this day and age when time is at a premium and more and more mixes and frozen cakes come on to the market? Because, when one has time to spare, few things are more soothing and satisfying than employing the old-fashioned skills of baking in the home. The results, moreover, can be extremely rewarding . . . home baking has a way of strengthening the bonds of family life.

The economics of home baking are also appealing with larger families, particularly where children make hungry demands on biscuits.

But be prepared . . . home baking makes Olivers of your family and friends—they always come back for more.

BREAD AND BUNS 1

Home breadmaking is now enjoying a revival as more people become disenchanted with the sliced and wrapped packets of "cottonwool" on sale in the shops.

Yeast cookery is adaptable and can easily be fitted into the household routine. It is also rather nice to be able to pull, punch, stretch and pummel dough instead of the light handling needed for other forms of baking such as pastry and cakes. The aroma of freshly baked bread or yeast buns will make you so popular with the family that any extra trouble will seem worthwhile. Please note that metric measurements are given in brackets. Please read the notes on page 92.

Using yeast opens up a whole new range of recipes. However the comment which is made most frequently about yeast cookery is that it takes too long! It does take a long time but you don't have to stand over it all the time and you can adapt the rising times to suit yourself. A warm temperature (not hot) hastens the process, a very cool temperature, e.g. in the refrigerator, lengthens the time of rising. Here is all the information you need for household baking. If yeast cookery is unfamiliar to you, read this through, before attempting each recipe.

YEAST

Use fresh or dried yeast—brewer's yeast is *not* for baking!

1 ounce fresh yeast = $\frac{1}{2}$ ounce or 1 level tablespoon dried yeast. Fresh yeast is obtainable from many bakers. Store in a loosely tied polythene bag. It should remain fresh for 4 to 5 days in a cold place, up to 1 month in a refrigerator and up to 1 year if it is tightly wrapped in a deep freeze.

Dried yeast is just as good as fresh if properly used. Dissolve 1 teaspoon sugar in a cup of warm water taken from the liquid in the recipe. Sprinkle the dried yeast on top and leave for at least 10 minutes when it will start to be frothy. Dried yeast can be bought at most chemists, some grocery stores and supermarkets, and of course at health food stores. It should keep for about 6 months in a cool place if it is in a container with a tightly fitting lid. Use the correct quantity of yeast—in other words follow the recipe. Too much yeast will result in a poor texture and yeast flavour.

It is possible to cream yeast with sugar, but bakers do not do this since it tends to destroy some of the yeast cells.

TEMPERATURE

Cold merely retards the growth of yeast and yeast doughs. Extreme heat will destroy the yeast, therefore do not put your dough to rise in a low oven as anything over 110°F, 43°C will have this effect. Average room temperature is all that is necessary for yeast cookery. Yeast doughs should rise away from draughts.

FLOUR

Strong plain flour is best for yeast recipes as it absorbs liquid easily. It develops easily into a firm elastic dough with kneading. Some flours are marked strong but if you cannot find strong flour use good quality plain flour.

Soft flour is used for cakes, pastry and biscuits. *All self-raising flour is soft.*

Flour should be stored in a cool dry place. Keep the flour in the bag on a cool dry airy shelf. If kitchen is steamy keep in a tin or jar with a lid. Fold over the top of the bag after use to prevent crumbs etc. from getting into the flour. White flour keeps well but brown flour should be used up quickly (within a few weeks). Do not add new flour to old stock.

LIQUID

Roughly, less than ½ pint (3 decilitres, 284 millilitres) liquid to 1 pound (450 grams) flour is an average quantity, but this depends on the flour and the general conditions. After all the liquid has been added, if the dough is too soft add a little extra flour for easier handling.

KNEADING

It is necessary to knead dough thoroughly for good rising. Pull and pummel dough for at least 5 minutes until it is firm and springy to the touch. If using the dough hook on a mixer use at low speed for 2–3 minutes. Put rising unshaped dough in a greased plastic container with a lid or cover with a polythene bag. If left in a mixing bowl grease the bowl and cover with polythene.
Rising will take:
 45–60 minutes in a warm place
 2 hours at room temperature
 12 hours in a cold room or larder
 24 hours in a refrigerator.

Some recipes suggest 'knocking back' the dough after the first rising for a better texture. After this step re-shape the dough and allow to rise again in the loaf tins. The final proving takes 30–40 minutes for bread, 15–20 minutes for buns.

When dough is shaped put in greased loaf tins or shape for rolls etc. on a greased baking sheet. To keep dough in refrigerator place in a large lightly-tied greased polythene bag. Dough will keep for 24 hours in a refrigerator but remember to bring back to room temperature before using.

WHITE BREAD

For 1 large loaf, 2 small loaves or 18 rolls.
DRY MIX:
 1½ pounds (675 grams) plain flour
 1 level teaspoon salt
 ½ ounce lard (15 grams) rubbed into flour and salt
YEAST LIQUID:
 Blend ½ ounce (15 grams) fresh yeast into ¾ pint (4½ decilitres, 426 millilitres) water; or dissolve 1 teaspoon sugar in ¾ pint (4½ decilitres) warm water (110°F, 43°C). Sprinkle on 2 level teaspoons dried yeast, leave until frothy, about 10 minutes.

Step 1. Mix dry ingredients with yeast liquid using a wooden spoon or fork. Work to a firm dough, adding extra flour if needed, until sides of the bowl are clean.

Step 2. Turn dough onto a lightly floured board or table and knead thoroughly to stretch and develop dough. To do this fold dough towards you then push down and away with palm of the hand. Continue until dough feels firm and elastic and no longer sticky, approximately 10 minutes. Shape dough into a ball.

Step 3. Place in a lightly greased large polythene bag loosely tied, or a large saucepan with a lid, and allow to rise until double in size and dough springs back when pressed with a floured finger.

Choose the rising time to fit in with the day's plans. Best results are achieved by a slow rise.

Quick rise: 45–60 minutes in a warm place
Slower rise: 2 hours at average room temperature
Overnight rise: Up to 12 hours in cold larder or room, or up to 24 hours in a refrigerator

Refrigerator-risen dough must be returned to room temperature before shaping. Turn risen dough onto lightly floured board or table. Flatten firmly with knuckles to knock out air bubbles then knead to make dough firm and ready for shaping.

Note: When kneading or shaping bread use only a little flour. Too much flour spoils the colour of the crust.

Step 4. For a large loaf grease a 2-pound loaf tin. Stretch dough into an oblong the same width as tin. Fold into three and turn in ends and place in tin.

For 2 small loaves divide dough into two and shape as above. Place in two greased 1-pound loaf tins.

For 18 rolls lightly grease a baking sheet. Divide dough into 18 equal pieces, 2 ounces (30 grams) each. Roll each piece into a ball using palm of hand. Using an unfloured board and a little flour on palm of hand press down hard at first, then ease up. Place rolls on baking sheet, about 1 inch apart.

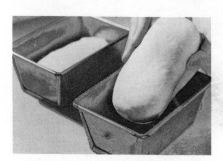

Step 5. To rise again, or prove, place tins or baking sheet inside a lightly greased polythene bag and leave to rise until dough comes to top of tin and springs back when pressed with a floured finger. Leave for 1–1½ hours at room temperature or longer in a refrigerator.

Step 6. Remove polythene, bake loaves in centre of a hot oven, 450 F, 230°C or Gas Mark 8, for 30–40 minutes, rolls for 15–20 minutes, until well risen and golden brown. Remove loaf from tin or rolls from baking sheet and cool on a wire tray.

Cooked loaves shrink slightly from sides of tin and sound hollow when tapped underneath with the knuckles.

PIZZA

Baking time: 20–30 minutes

- 1 pound (450 grams) white dough which has had 1 rising
- 4 6-inch sandwich tins or 2 small Swiss roll tins
- oil (preferably olive) for brushing

FILLING:

- 8 ounces (225 grams) cheese
- 1 large can Italian peeled tomatoes
- 2 tablespoons tomato purée
- 1 clove garlic, crushed
- 1 teaspoon fresh or dried thyme, oregano, marjoram or basil
- 1 can anchovy fillets
- stoned and halved black olives

Roll the risen dough into a long strip. Brush with oil and roll up like a Swiss roll. Repeat this step 3 times. Divide the dough into the portions required for the oiled tins being used. Roll dough to fit tin and press in with the knuckles. Brush over with oil, cover with alternate layers of tomato and herb mixture with cheese. Finish with grated cheese or cheese slices, anchovies and black olives. Stand in a cool place for about 30 minutes. Bake in the second top shelf of a hot oven, 450°F, 230°C or Gas Mark 8, for 20–30 minutes.

Experiment with your own favourite filling, e.g. ham, bacon, tuna fish.

ENRICHED BREAD

Baking time: 50 minutes

- 1 pound (450 grams) plain flour
- 1 level teaspoon salt
- 1 level teaspoon sugar
- ½ ounce (15 grams) fresh yeast or
- 1 teaspoon dried yeast
- scant ½ pint (2½ decilitres, 280 millilitres) warm milk
- 2 ounces (50 grams) margarine or butter
- 1 egg

Mix 5 ounces (150 grams) of flour together with the yeast, sugar and milk. Allow to stand in a warm place until frothy. Sieve the flour that remains with the salt and rub in the butter or margarine. Add egg then combine the two mixtures. Knead thoroughly for about 10 minutes on a lightly floured board. It may be sticky to begin with but no extra flour should be added.

Put the dough in an oiled polythene bag tied loosely and allow to rise until the dough springs back when pressed.

Turn the dough on to a floured board, knead lightly and divide half.

To shape the plait: Divide dough into two and roll two 12- by 14-inch pieces. Arrange the two strips in a cross on the board. Take two opposite ends of each strip and cross them over in the centre. Cross each strip alternately 2 or 3 times. Then gather the short ends together and lay the plait on its side on a floured baking sheet.

Bake in a hot oven 375°F, 190°C or Gas Mark 5, on the middle shelf for 45–50 minutes or until the loaves sound hollow when tapped and are lightly browned. Cool on a wire tray.

Makes 1 plait loaf.

WHEATMEAL BREAD

Baking time: 30 minutes

- 1¾ ounce (50 grams) yeast
- scant 1½ pints (8 decilitres) water
- 3 pounds (1 kilo 350 grams) flour
- ¾ ounce (scant 25 grams) salt
- 1 ounce (25 grams) fat

Work the yeast with half the tepid water. Mix the flour with the salt. Melt the fat, then make a well in the middle of the flour and pour in the yeast and fat and gradually work all together with the remaining lukewarm water. Knead well and put the dough to rise for about 35–40 minutes in a warm place until it has about doubled its size.

Divide into 6 and shape into rolls. Place in lightly greased 1-pound loaf tins or onto baking sheets. Prove for at least 30–40 minutes. Bake in a hot oven, 440°F, 225°C or Gas Mark 8, for about 30 minutes.

MALT BREAD: Add 2 ounces warmed malt to the flour with the liquid, fat and yeast.

Enriched bread

a

Wheatmeal bread

ROUND LOAVES: Place the two balls of dough on large baking sheet prepared as above. With a sharp knife score loaves, making 4 shallow cuts, 1 inch apart, across top, then making 4 crosswise cuts. Then brush, rise and bake as above.
Makes 6 1-pound loaves or 3 2-pound loaves.

FLOWERPOT LOAVES

Baking time: 30–40 minutes

- 1 pound (450 grams) wheatmeal flour, or a mixture of wheatmeal and plain flour
- ¼ ounce (7 grams) lard or margarine
- 2 level teaspoons sugar
- 2 level teaspoons salt
- ½ ounce (15 grams) yeast or 2 level teaspoons dried yeast
- ½ pint (3 decilitres, 284 millilitres) water

To make dough with fresh yeast:
Mix the flours, salt and sugar together in a bowl; rub in fat. Blend yeast in the water and add all at once. Mix to a soft, scone-like dough (adding more flour if necessary) which leaves the bowl clean.

To make the dough with dried yeast:
Dissolve a teaspoon of the sugar in a cupful of water used in the recipe (to get the best result this water should be warmed to 110°F, 43°C, or hand hot), then sprinkle dried yeast on top. Leave till frothy, about 10 minutes. Add with remaining liquid to the flour, salt and remaining sugar. Mix to a soft, scone-like dough. Knead the dough thoroughly on a lightly floured surface. Divide into 2 pieces.

To make loaves:
Shape each piece to half fill a well-greased 1-pound loaf tin or 4- to 5-inch flower pot. Brush tops with salt and water and sprinkle with cornflakes or cracked wheat. Put to rise, inside a large greased polythene bag, loosely tied, until the dough has doubled in size and springs back when lightly pressed with a floured finger. Remove bag. Bake on middle shelf of a hot oven, 450°F, 230°C or Gas Mark 8, for 30–40 minutes.

Note: Grease the flower pot well before using and bake it empty in a hot oven several times. This prevents the loaf from sticking.
Makes 2 Flowerpot loaves.

Flowerpot loaf

SCOTTISH BAPS

Cooking time: 15 minutes

- ¾ ounce (scant 25 grams) yeast
- 1 level teaspoon caster sugar
- scant ½ pint (2½ decilitres) milk and water
- 12 ounces (325 grams) plain flour
- ½ teaspoon salt
- 1½ ounces (40 grams) cooking fat

Cream the yeast together with the sugar and blend this with the mixture of milk and water. Sieve the flour and salt then rub in the fat. Make a well in the centre of the flour and pour in the yeast liquid.

Allow the mixture to prove like this for 15 minutes until the middle begins to froth. Knead the dough till smooth, grease and flour the bowl, place the dough in the bowl and cover with a polythene bag. Allow to prove for about 1 hour.

Knead the dough and form into small ovals, and place on a warm greased baking sheet. Allow enough room for the mixture to expand. Brush the baps over with milk and dust with flour, and allow to prove for a further 15 minutes. Dust again with flour and press the tops down with the palm of the hand. Bake in the pre-heated oven, 450°F, 230°C or Gas Mark 8, for about 15 minutes.

These rolls are served at breakfast time in Scotland. They are delicious warm and they make perfect sandwiches.
Makes 12 baps.

CROISSANTS

Baking time: 12–15 minutes

Anyone who has breakfasted in France on delicious croissants and coffee will vouch for this as an ideal alternative to a cooked breakfast. Try the croissants with apricot or peach jam for an extra treat.

1 pound (450 grams) plain flour
1½ level teaspoons salt
½ ounce (15 grams) margarine or butter
generous ½ ounce (15 grams) yeast
½ pint (3 decilitres) water and milk
1 egg
6 ounces (175 grams) butter

Sieve the flour and salt, add the melted butter. Add a spoonful of the warmed milk and water to the yeast, and cream together. Now add the creamed yeast and remaining liquid to the flour. Knead well and leave in a warm place for nearly an hour.

Step 1. Turn on to a floured board, knead lightly, then roll out into an oblong.

Step 2. Put a third of the butter on the oblong in small pats using the same method as for flaky pastry (see page 76).

Step 3. Fold one third up, one third down, turn, and roll out again into an oblong. Repeat this step twice using the remaining butter. Each time reshape the dough to a long strip by gently pressing with the rolling pin.

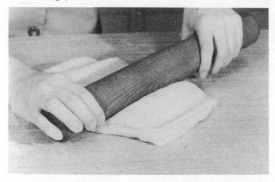

Step 4. Cut the dough into triangular shapes using the simple ruler method shown in the picture.

Step 5. Roll and shape the croissants as shown. Place on lightly greased warmed trays. Prove for 15 minutes in a warm place then brush over with beaten egg.

Step 6. Bake in a pre-heated oven, 450°F, 230°C or Gas Mark 8, for about 12–15 minutes.
Makes 8 croissants.

CINNAMON ORANGE SWIRL

Baking time: 35 minutes

½ ounce (15 grams) fresh yeast
2 tablespoons water
8 ounces (225 grams) plain flour
1 level teaspoon salt
1 tablespoon sugar
1 egg, beaten
peel of 1½ medium or 1 large orange, minced or finely chopped to a pulp (3 ounces, 75 grams), or the juice and rind of half an orange

FILLING:

½ tablespoon cinnamon ⎫
1 ounce (25 grams) ⎬ mixed together
brown sugar ⎭

DECORATION:

glacé icing

Prepare yeast: Blend yeast with water; or dissolve ½ teaspoon sugar in 2 tablespoons warm water (110°F, 43°C); sprinkle with ½ level tablespoon dried yeast. Leave until frothy, about 10 minutes.

Mix together the yeast liquid with flour, salt, sugar, eggs and orange pulp or juice and rind. Work to a firm dough, adding 2–3 extra tablespoons warm water if required. Turn out and knead well until the dough feels smooth and elastic. Put the dough to rise in a lightly greased polythene bag loosely tied, or in an 8-inch saucepan with lid. Leave to rise until double in size, about 1 hour in a warm place.

Turn out the risen dough and knead lightly for 2 minutes. Roll to a rectangle 6 inches by 13. Brush lightly with water and sprinkle on the cinnamon sugar. Roll up as for a Swiss roll and place in a greased polythene bag; leave to rise until the dough springs back when pressed lightly with a floured finger, about 30 minutes in a warm place. Remove polythene. Bake on a greased baking sheet in a fairly hot oven, 400°F, 200 C, Gas Mark 6, for 30–35 minutes or in a greased 1-pound loaf tin. When cold, ice with glacé icing. Makes 1 Cinnamon roll.

BARA BRITH

Baking time: 1½–2 hours

1½ pounds (675 grams) plain flour
6 ounces (175 grams) lard or butter
½ teaspoon salt
6 ounces (175 grams) sugar
½ teaspoon mixed spice
8 ounces (225 grams) stoned raisins
4 ounces (100 grams) candied peel
½ ounce (15 grams) yeast
½ pint (3 decilitres) milk
1 egg

Sieve the flour then rub in the fat until mixture is like fine breadcrumbs. Add other dry ingredients and mix well. Mix the yeast with the warmed milk. Make a well in the centre of the flour mixture and drop in the egg and yeast mixture. Mix well to a soft dough. Cover with a polythene bag and prove until mixture has doubled its size.

Flour the board then knead the dough lightly. Grease 2 1-pound loaf tins, divide the dough in 2, place in tins. Allow to rise again for 15 minutes.

Bake in the centre of a fairly hot oven, 400°F, 200°C or Gas Mark 5, for 1½ hours. Reduce heat to 325°F, 160°C, Gas Mark 3, after 30 minutes. Serve buttered when cold.
Makes 2 1-pound loaves.

Bara brith

Cinnamon swirl

SCANDINAVIAN BUNS

Baking time: 10–15 minutes

There is an old custom in Scandinavia that on St. Lucia's Day (December 13th) the eldest daughter of the house, dressed in white and with a wreath of lighted candles on her head, wakes the family to a breakfast of these buns.

1 ounce (25 grams) fresh yeast
¼ pint (1½ decilitres) water
¼ pint (1½ decilitres) milk
⅛ teaspoon saffron powder
2 ounces (50 grams) butter or margarine
3 ounces (75 grams) sugar
1 pound 2 ounces (½ kilo) plain flour
1 level teaspoon salt
1 egg
2 ounces (50 grams) raisins

Blend yeast with water, or dissolve 1 teaspoon sugar in ¼ pint warm water (110°F, 43°C), sprinkle 1 level tablespoon dried yeast on top, and leave for 10 minutes till frothy.

Heat milk and mix in saffron. Add butter or margarine and sugar and stir until fat has melted. Cool. In a second warmed bowl mix the flour with salt (reserving 2 tablespoons of flour for kneading). Add milk mixture, yeast liquid, egg and raisins, and beat well together to make a soft dough. Turn out onto remaining flour on a board and knead flour with dough till you get a smooth elastic ball. Put to rise in a lightly greased polythene bag or an 8-inch saucepan with lid at room temperature for about 2 hours. (A slow rise gives better results with this dough.) Turn the dough out onto a lightly floured board. Knead and divide into three pieces (keep the dough you are not working with covered), and make a variety of shapes as follows.

WAGGON WHEELS: Divide into 8 pieces and roll each into a strip 9 inches long. Lightly flour a baking sheet, lay 2 strips side by side, pinch centres together, and coil ends.

LUCIA BUNS: Divide as above. Roll into 9-inch strips. On baking tin, cross the strips to make an 'X'. Curl each end into a small coil.

TWISTS: Divide as above, roll into 9-inch strips and shape each strip on baking tin into an 'S'. Curl each end as before.

1. Cut the buns out with a scone cutter.
2. Pipe the custard on the buns after baking.

Press a raisin into the centre of each coil. Put baking tin in a lightly greased polythene bag. Leave to rise in a warm place until buns are light and puffy, about 20 minutes. Brush with an egg mixed with a little water and 1 teaspoon sugar, and bake near the top of a fairly hot oven, 400°F, 200°C or Gas Mark 6, for 10–15 minutes until golden brown.

Makes 24 buns altogether.

HOT CROSS BUNS

Baking time:

1 pound (450 grams) plain flour
1 teaspoon mixed spice
½ teaspoon salt
2 ounces (50 grams) margarine
6 ounces (175 grams) currants
½ ounce (15 grams) chopped peel
2 ounces (50 grams) caster sugar
½ ounce (15 grams) dried yeast
   (1 ounce fresh)
12 tablespoons milk
1 egg
CROSSES:
2 ounces (50 grams) shortcrust pastry
   see page 66

Warm a mixing bowl and sieve in flour and spice. Rub in the margarine until the consistency is of fine breadcrumbs. Add fruit and sugar, reserving 1 teaspoon caster sugar for the yeast. Cream together the yeast and sugar then add warmed milk; alternatively, make up dried yeast as directed on packet. Add the egg to the yeast and milk, mix the dough with your hand until it is fairly soft. Turn out on to a floured board and knead for a few minutes. Return to the bowl and cover with a cloth or polythene sheet. Allow to double in size: this will take over an hour in a warm place. Turn out the risen dough, knead lightly and divide into 12 equal balls. Shape into buns and allow to rise on a greased baking sheet covered with cloth or polythene for about 25 minutes. Make crosses (for

alternative see below), brush the top of the buns with a little milk and place a cross on each. Bake for 15–20 minutes in a hot oven, 425°F or Gas Mark 7. Boil the glaze for a few minutes and brush on while the buns are still hot.

Alternatively mix 1 tablespoon milk and ½ teaspoon vanilla essence with 3 ounces (80 grams) sieved icing sugar. Pipe crosses onto buns as shown in picture.
Makes 12 buns.

1. Pack the dough over the butter or margarine. Seal the edges and roll out into a rectangle.

DANISH PASTRIES

Baking time: 20–30 minutes
10 ounces (275 grams) plain flour
1 ounce (25 grams) yeast
¾ ounce (scant 25 grams) sugar
1 egg
4 tablespoons milk
4½ ounces (125 grams) margarine

Mix the yeast, sugar, and egg together in a bowl with the milk. Sieve in the flour. Knead until you have a smooth dough. Sprinkle the table with flour and place the dough on it.

Form the margarine into a square and place it on the dough. Pack the dough up over the margarine to form a square parcel. Roll out to a rectangle about ½ inch thick. Fold in three as for flaky pastry. Turn the dough once to the left so that the fold is to the left hand. Roll, fold, and turn twice more. Leave to rest for 15 minutes. Roll out and cut into rounds, squares and triangles which can be filled or sprinkled with the following.

FILLINGS:
Confectioner's custard, jam, apples and nuts, almond paste, mixtures of dried fruit, spice mixed with caster sugar.
Makes 22 pastries approximately.

DANISH PASTRY TRIANGLES: After the dough has rested, roll it out and cut into 20 squares. Put a dot of margarine into the centre of each square. Fold over to form a triangle. Press the edges well together. Make 5 or 6 slashes in each with a knife.

Place on a baking sheet. Leave to rise for 15 minutes. Brush with beaten egg. Sprinkle the centre of each with a few chopped nuts. Bake in a moderate oven, 350°F, 175°C or Gas Mark 4 for about 20–30 minutes. When cool spread each pastry with glacé icing.
Makes 20 triangles.

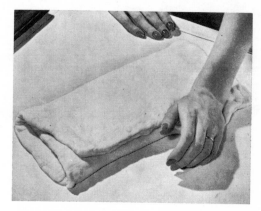

2. Fold into three, as if making flaky pastry.

3. Finished Danish pastries in different shapes with various fillings.

Colourful tea-time treat: German Stollen.

GERMAN STOLLEN

Baking time: 45–55 minutes

- 2 ounces (50 grams) plain flour
- ½ teaspoon sugar
- ¼ ounce (7 grams) fresh yeast, or
- 1 level teaspoon dried yeast
- ¼ pint (1½ decilitres) warm milk
- 3 ounces (75 grams) butter
- 2 ounces (50 grams) caster sugar)
- 1 egg
- 6 ounces (150 grams) plain flour
- ½ teaspoon salt
- 3 ounces (75 grams) raisins
- 1 ounce (25 grams) chopped almonds
- grated rind of half a lemon
- 1 ounce (25 grams) mixed peel

FILLING:

- ½ ounce (15 grams) melted butter
- 3 ounces (75 grams) chopped glacé
  cherries, or 3 tablespoons mincemeat

DECORATION:

- glacé icing, cherries and angelica

Mix the 2-ounce portion of flour, ½ teaspoon sugar, yeast and warm milk to a batter in a large bowl. Leave the batter to become frothy for 20–30 minutes in a warm place. Cream butter and sugar, add the egg and beat well. Add creamed mixture to the frothy batter with the rest of the flour, salt, fruit, nuts and peel. Mix to make a dough. Cover the bowl with a lightly greased polythene bag. Leave to rise until double in size, 1½–2 hours in a warm place, longer in a cool one. Turn the dough on to a lightly floured board and knead well. Shape into an oval about 12 inches by 8 inches and brush with melted butter. Spread on the filling and fold over lengthwise so that the top layer is 1 inch from the edge of the bottom. Put the Stollen on a floured baking sheet and cover with greased polythene. Allow to rise until dough springs back when pressed with a lightly floured finger (for about ¾ hour in a warm place). Remove the polythene. Brush loaf with melted butter and bake in a moderate oven, 350°F, 170°C or Gas Mark 4, for 45–55 minutes.

When cool, decorate with glacé icing, cherries and angelica.

Makes 1 Stollen.

APRICOT AND WALNUT LOAF

Baking time: 40–45 minutes
For this loaf you can use half the quantity of the wheatmeal bread recipe (see page 11).

12 ounces (325 grams) wheatmeal dough which has had 1 rising
4 ounces (160 grams) chopped, dried apricots
2 ounces (50 grams) chopped walnuts
1 ounce (25 grams) sugar
1 ounce (25 grams) margarine

TOPPING:
1 ounce (25 grams) margarine
1 ounce (25 grams) sugar
1½ tablespoons plain flour

OR:
crushed cornflakes may be used on top of the dough

Work all ingredients together in a basin, with one hand until they are evenly mixed. Fill the prepared 1-pound loaf tin and put into a polythene bag until the dough rises to within ½ inch of the top of the tin. Allow to rise for 1 hour in a warm place or longer if temperature is low.

Cover with topping and bake on the middle shelf of a pre-heated oven, 400°F, 204 C or Gas Mark 6, for 40–45 minutes. Leave the loaf in the tin for about 10 minutes then cool on a wire tray. Makes 1 1-pound loaf.

TEA RING

Baking time:
6 ounces (175 grams) plain flour
¼ teaspoon salt
½ ounce (15 grams) sugar
scant ½ ounce (15 grams) fresh yeast (or 1 teaspoon dried yeast)
scant ¼ pint (1½ decilitres) warm milk
½ egg

FILLING:
1 ounce (25 grams) caster sugar
1 ounce (25 grams) ground almonds
hot water to mix

ICING:
3 ounces (75 grams) icing sugar, sieved
warm water

Mix flour and salt, add most of the sugar. Cream the yeast with 1 teaspoon sugar, add warm milk and egg then mix to a dough. Knead lightly then allow to rise in a warm place until it doubles in size. Roll out in an oblong, spread on filling, damp edges and roll up. Form into a ring and prove on a greased baking sheet for 15 minutes. Bake in a hot oven, 425°F, 220 C or Gas Mark 7, for 10 minutes. Reduce heat to 375 F, 190 C or Gas Mark 5 and bake until golden brown. Spread with icing and sprinkle with chopped almonds, cherries and angelica.
Makes 1 ring.

Tea Ring

CHELSEA BUNS

Baking time: 25 minutes

    8 ounces (225 grams) plain flour
    pinch of salt
    2 ounces (50 grams) lard or margarine
    1½ tablespoons caster sugar
    5 tablespoons milk
    ½ ounce (15 grams) yeast
    1 egg
    ½ ounce (15 grams) mixed peel

Sieve the flour and salt. Rub in the fat, or melt it and add it to the milk. Cream the yeast with ½ teaspoon caster sugar and add the warm milk. Add the yeast, milk and egg to the flour. Beat well with a wooden spoon. Put the dough in a warm place to rise until double its size. Roll it out into a 10-inch square. Brush with melted lard. Sprinkle with currants, sugar and mixed peel. Roll up firmly and cut into rounds 1 inch thick. Place the rounds closely together in a 7-inch sandwich tin, with the cut sides uppermost.

Stand in a warm place for 20–30 minutes or until the buns almost reach the top of the tin. Then brush with egg. Bake at 450°F, 230°C or Gas Mark 8, for 25 minutes.

While still hot, brush the buns with a glaze made by boiling 1 tablespoon of granulated sugar with 1 tablespoon of water for 1 minute. Sprinkle the glazed buns with caster sugar. Alternatively the roll may be placed in a loaf tin, allow to rise and bake as for yeast fruit bread.

Makes 10 buns.

Roll up firmly like a Swiss roll then cut into a round, 1″ thick.

COFFEE RING

Baking time: 30 minutes
- 8 ounces (225 grams) plain flour
- pinch of salt
- 2 ounces (50 grams) caster sugar
- ½ ounce (15 grams) yeast
- 6 tablespoons milk and water
- 2 tablespoons chocolate chips or Polka Dots
- 1 ounce (25 grams) butter or margarine
- 1 egg
- 1 tablespoon coffee essence
- melted butter

Sieve the flour and the salt in a warmed bowl. Cream the yeast with 1 teaspoon sugar and mix with warmed liquid. Add this liquid to about a third of the flour (without mixing) and allow to rise until sponge breaks through. Rub the butter into remaining flour and add remaining sugar. Gradually beat in the egg, coffee essence and then the yeast mixture. Add chocolate chips and knead thoroughly with the hand; allow to rise in a warm place. When it has doubled its size knead lightly again. Roll the dough into an oblong, roll up and form roll into a ring. Allow to prove on a greased baking sheet for 25 minutes. Bake in a hot oven, 450°F, 230°C or Gas Mark 8, for about 30 minutes. Finish with coffee glacé icing.
Makes 1 ring.

BABAS AU RHUM

Baking time: 10–12 minutes
- ¼ ounce (7 grams) yeast
- 1 ounce (25 grams) caster sugar
- 5 tablespoons warmed milk
- 4 ounces (100 grams) plain flour
- pinch of salt
- 2 eggs
- 1 ounce (25 grams) butter
- 1 ounce (25 grams) sultanas
- 1 ounce (25 grams) currants
- 1 ounce (25 grams) glacé cherries, chopped

SYRUP:
- ½ pint (3 decilitres) water
- 6 ounces (175 grams) sugar
- 3–4 tablespoons rum

FILLING AND DECORATION:
- whipped cream
- cherries and angelica

Coffee ring

Cream the yeast with 1 teaspoon sugar then add a little of the warm milk. Sieve the flour and salt into a warm mixing bowl and make a well in the centre of the flour. Pour in the yeast mixture and sprinkle with a little flour. Cover with a polythene bag and allow to stand in a warm place for 15 minutes or until the sponge breaks through. Add beaten eggs, sugar, remaining warm milk and melted butter. Beat well for some minutes then add the fruit. Grease the baba tins (individual flan tins or deep patty tins). Half fill the tins with mixture and allow to rise to the top of the tins. Bake on the second shelf of a hot oven, 425°F, 220°C or Gas Mark 7. Make the syrup by melting the sugar in water and then allow to reduce by boiling rapidly. Turn the babas out of the tins when baked and prick with a clean skewer. Add the rum to the syrup and pour over the babas. Serve hot or cold, decorated with whipped cream, cherries, angelica and flaked almonds.

Savarin

For Savarin use the mixture as for Babas au Rhum but omit the dried fruit. Cook in a savarin tin. Rum or Kirsch can be used in the syrup. The savarin may be finished for Babas au Rhum with cream or filled with fruit, e.g. strawberries or peaches. Cream can be used for decoration or handed separately.

DOUGHNUTS

100g SOFT BROWN SUGAR

22

50g BUTTER

MIX

ADD I EGG MIX

450g PLAIN FLOUR

½ TBL SPOON
BAKING POWDER

½ TSP CINNAMON

I TSP VANILLA

PINCH SALT

MIX

FRIDGE 2HRS

DEEP FRY

Delicious savarin for dessert.

DOUGHNUTS

Cooking time: about 30 minutes
12 ounces (325 grams) plain flour
pinch of salt
½ ounce (15 grams) yeast
6 tablespoons milk and water
(blood heat)
2 ounces (50 grams) sugar

Sieve the flour and salt into a warmed bowl. Cream
the yeast with a little sugar then add the liquid.
Sprinkle with flour and allow to stand in a warm
place until it bubbles. Rub margarine into sieved
flour then add sugar. Work in the yeast to the
flour kneading thoroughly. Allow dough to rise in
a warm place until it has doubled its size. Roll out
the dough about ½ inch thick. Cut out rings with
pastry cutters.

Allow to rise for a further 15 minutes. Heat oil
or cooking fat (clean) in a deep saucepan. Test
with a square of bread (1 minute to turn bread
golden brown). Put in the doughnuts and cook
for about 5 minutes. Drain on absorbent paper, toss
in caster sugar.
Makes 16 doughnuts.

Jam Doughnuts

Form mixture into small balls. Make a deep hole
for the jam, seal over and allow to prove. Cook for
5–10 minutes.

Ring and jam doughnuts

SCONES

I am now going to deal with the quick tea-time recipes such as scones and tea breads without yeast. Scones should be eaten the same day, tea breads or loaves you can store for some days. Left-over scones can be heated in the oven for a few minutes the next day, but they are at their best when eaten fresh. My family enjoy them hot with the butter melting in the middle. If you are new to scone baking here are a few points to bear in mind. Rub in the fat with the tips of the fingers and handle the mixture lightly.

Make sure that you use the correct amount of raising agent.

The basic dough must be slightly sticky—use enough liquid to make the mixture into a softer consistency than a pastry dough.

Roll the scones on a floured board; handle very lightly. You may even prefer to flatten them with your hand.

Scones are always baked near the top of a hot oven and they will take around 8–15 minutes according to size and thickness.

Scones can be left in the refrigerator for some time before cooking. However it is best not to leave them too long in a warm room before cooking.

Freshly baked scones are ideal for tea-time.

OVEN SCONES

Baking time: 10 minutes
  8 ounces (200 grams) self-raising flour
  2 teaspoons baking powder
  pinch of salt
  2 ounces (50 grams) margarine
  1 ounce (25 grams) caster sugar
  scant ¼ pint (1 decilitre) milk

Step 1. Sieve the flour, baking powder and salt in a mixing bowl. Rub in the fat until the mixture has the texture of fine breadcrumbs. Stir in the sugar. Quickly mix in the milk to form a fairly soft dough.

Step 2. Knead the dough lightly on a floured board and roll out to ½-inch thickness.

Step 3. Cut into rounds with a fluted cutter and place on a baking sheet. Allow to rest in a cool place if possible for 20 minutes. Brush the tops with egg or milk and bake in a hot oven, 425°F, 220°C or Gas Mark 7, for 10–12 minutes. Cool on a wire tray.

Makes about 10 scones.

If your scones are not successful, here are several faults which may be causing failure:
1. If the scones do not rise well: insufficient raising agent, oven too cool, mixture over-kneaded.
2. If the scones are rough and leathery: mixture over-kneaded.
3. If the texture is hard and close: insufficient liquid used in mixing.
4. If the scones are pale and doughy: cooking time too short, oven too cool, cooked on low shelf in oven.

CHEESE SCONES

Baking time: about 12 minutes
  8 ounces (200 grams) self-raising flour
  2 level teaspoons baking powder
  ½ level teaspoon salt
  2 ounces (50 grams) margarine or butter
  3 tablespoons grated cheese
  ¼ level teaspoon dry mustard
  ¼ pint (1½ decilitres) milk

Pre-heat the oven to 425 F, 220°C, Gas Mark 7. Sieve the dry ingredients into a bowl and then rub the fat into the mixture until it resembles fine breadcrumbs. Add the grated cheese and then the milk and mix with a round bladed knife to a soft dough. Turn the dough on to a floured table and knead lightly with the tips of the fingers. Roll out quite thickly (about ½ inch) and cut into rounds. Press remaining pieces of dough together with the finger tips and cut as before. Bake on the second top shelf of a pre-heated oven for about 12 minutes depending on the thickness of the scones. Makes 8–12 scones depending on the size of cutter used.

SCOTTISH TREACLE SCONES

Baking time: 15 minutes
  1 pound (400 grams) plain flour
  1 teaspoon bicarbonate of soda
  ½ teaspoon cream of tartar
  1 teaspoon ground cinnamon
  1 teaspoon mixed spice
  ½ teaspoon salt
  2 ounces (50 grams) butter or margarine
  2 teaspoons sugar
  2 tablespoons black treacle
  ½ pint (3 decilitres) milk

Preheat the oven to 425°F, 220°C or Gas Mark 7. Sieve together all dry ingredients except sugar. Rub in butter until mixture resembles fine breadcrumbs, then add sugar and treacle. Mix to a soft dough with milk. Turn out on a lightly floured board, knead lightly then roll out to ½-inch thickness. Cut into 3-inch triangles and brush tops with milk. Bake in a hot oven for about 15 minutes. Serve fresh from the oven while still warm with butter.

Makes 10 scones.

TREACLE SCONES

Baking time: 10 minutes
> **8 ounces (200 grams) self-raising flour**
> salt
> **1 teaspoon bicarbonate of soda**
> **1½ ounces (scant 50 grams) butter or margarine**
> **1½ tablespoons black treacle**
> **¼ pint (1½ decilitres) milk**

Preheat the oven to 425°F, 220°C or Gas Mark 7. Sieve the flour with the salt and baking powder. Rub in the fat until the mixture resembles fine breadcrumbs then add the milk and mix to a soft dough. Knead the mixture lightly and cut into triangles or rounds. Brush with egg. Bake in the oven for about 10 minutes.

Makes 8–10 scones.

WHOLEMEAL SCONES

Baking time: 12 minutes
> **4 ounces (100 grams) self-raising flour**
> salt
> **4 ounces (100 grams) wholemeal flour**
> **1½ teaspoons baking powder**
> **1 desertspoon caster sugar**
> **2 ounces (50 grams) butter or margarine**
> **¼ pint (1½ decilitres) milk**

Preheat the oven to 425 F, 220 C or Gas Mark 7. Sieve the flour with the salt then add wholemeal flour. Mix thoroughly before rubbing in the fat until mixture resembles fine breadcrumbs. Add sugar and mix thoroughly. Add the milk and mix with a palette knife or the tips of the fingers until soft dough is formed.

Turn the dough on to a floured board, knead lightly and form into a round. Cut the round into four. Place on a baking sheet, fitting the four pieces together to form the round again. Dust with flour and bake in the heated oven for 12 minutes. Serve with butter.

Makes 10 scones.

Try Scotch pancakes with Philadelphia cheese for tea-time.

KENT APPLE SCONE

Baking time: 30 minutes
> **2 medium cooking apples**
> **1 pound (450 grams) self-raising flour**
> **1 teaspoon salt**
> **2 level teaspoons baking powder**
> **4 ounces (125 grams) butter**
> **4 ounces (125 grams) caster sugar**
> scant ½ pint (2½ decilitres) cold milk
> **1 tablespoon sieved apricot jam**

Preheat the oven to 400 F, 200 C or Gas Mark 6. Peel, core and finely chop one apple. Sieve together the flour, salt and baking powder. Rub in butter, then add caster sugar and chopped apple. Mix to a soft but not sticky dough with milk. Roll out to 8-inch circle, about 1½ inches thick on floured baking sheet. Mark the top to make 8 wedges. Peel and core remaining apple and cut into thin slices. Brush top of scone with milk and arrange apple slices on top. Bake in a moderately hot oven for about 30 minutes. While still hot, brush apple slices with apricot jam. Serve warm with butter.

Makes 8 triangles.

SCOTCH PANCAKES (DROPPED SCONES)

> **8 ounces (200 grams) self-raising flour**
> **2 teaspoons baking powder**
> pinch of salt
> **1 ounce (25 grams) caster sugar**
> **1 egg**
> generous ¼ pint (1½ decilitres) milk

Sieve the flour and baking powder in a mixing bowl. Stir in the caster sugar. Make a well in the centre, drop in the egg and add some of the milk. Beat the batter until bubbles appear on the surface. Add the remaining milk and allow the batter to stand for at least ½ hour.

Cheese scones are just right for savoury tastes.

Stir once before using then preheat a girdle or strong frying-pan on a moderate heat. Allow to heat up slowly. Grease with a piece of dripping wrapped in muslin or greaseproof paper. Drop 3 or 4 desertspoons of the mixture on to the girdle or pan. Turn with a palette knife when bubbles appear on the surface. Cool on a wire tray and cover with a clean tea towel.
Makes 24 pancakes.

GIRDLE SCONES

Baking time: about 2 minutes each side
  8 ounces (200 grams) self-raising flour
  2 teaspoons baking powder
  pinch of salt
  1 ounce (25 grams) caster sugar
  2 ounces (50 grams) margarine
  scant ¼ pint (1 decilitre) milk
  2 heaped tablespoons currants

Proceed as for Step 1 for Oven Scones (see p. 24), adding the currants before kneading. Knead lightly and divide the dough into 4 pieces. Roll each portion out to a flat round about 6 inches in diameter and ¼-inch thick. Cut into 4 triangles. Heat the girdle or a thick frying pan on a medium heat and coat with melted fat. Place scones on the girdle and cook until golden brown and puffed up on top. Turn the scones and brown on the other side. Split the scones and serve hot with butter.

If your girdle scones are not successful, here are several faults which may be causing failure:
  tough and leathery—mixture over-kneaded;
  hard thick crust—overcooked;
  pale and doughy—undercooked.

RASPBERRY BUNS

Baking time: 15–20 minutes
  8 ounces (200 grams) self-raising flour
  pinch of salt
  3 ounces (75 grams) butter or margarine
  3 ounces (75 grams) caster sugar
  1 egg
  5 tablespoons milk
  finely grated rind of 1 lemon
  raspberry jam
  milk and sugar for coating

Preheat the oven to 400°F, 200°C or Gas Mark 6. Sieve the flour and salt together, cut the fat into small pieces, then rub into the flour. Add sugar and lemon rind. Beat the egg lightly with the milk and then mix all the ingredients together with a round bladed knife to form a fairly soft dough. Turn the dough onto a floured board and form into a long roll. Divide the roll into 12 portions and roll each into a ball with floured hands. Flatten each ball into a round shape. Place 1 small teaspoon jam in the centre of each round. Gather the edges of the round together to join in the centre, making sure the jam is completely sealed in. Turn the rounds upside down and place on a greased baking sheet. Brush the top of each round with milk and then sprinkle with sugar. Cook on the second top shelf of a fairly hot oven for 20 minutes. Cool on a wire tray.
Makes 12 buns.

COFFEE BUNS

Baking time: 15–20 minutes
- 4 ounces (100 grams) margarine
- 4 ounces (100 grams) caster sugar
- 2 eggs
- 5 ounces (125 grams) self-raising flour
- 1 tablespoon coffee essence
- 2 ounces (50 grams) Polka Dots

Preheat the oven to 375°F, 180°C or Gas Mark 5. Grease and flour bun tins. Cream the margarine and sugar until light and fluffy, then beat in whisked eggs a little at a time beating well. Sieve in flour and add Polka Dots; stir with a metal spoon. Add coffee essence. Fill bun tins two-thirds full and bake in a moderate oven for 15–20 minutes till risen and firm. Cool on a wire tray.
Makes 30 buns.

Date and walnut loaf can be served with or without glacé icing on top.

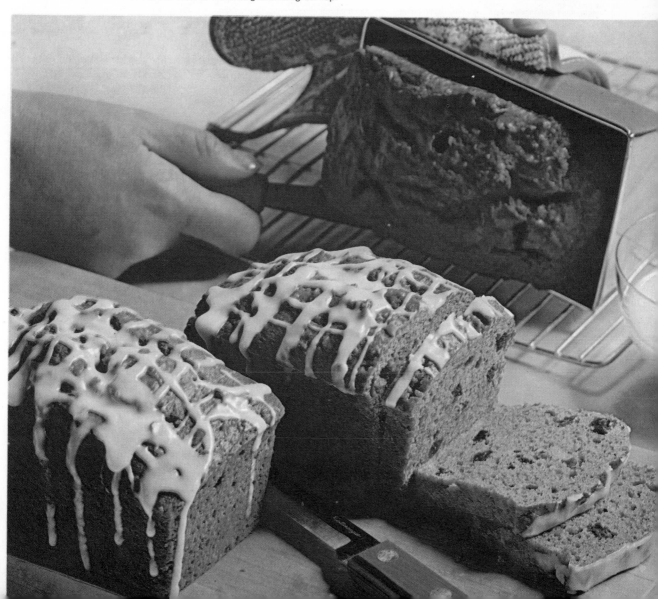

FRUIT LOAF

Baking time: 1½ hours
  8 ounces (200 grams) self-raising flour
  pinch of salt
  4 ounces (100 grams) margarine or butter
  4 ounces (100 grams) caster sugar
  2 eggs
  4(3) tablespoons milk
  4–8 ounces (100–200 grams) mixed dried
    fruit (sultanas, raisins and currants)

Preheat the oven to 350°F, 180°C or Gas Mark 4.
Sieve the flour and salt into a bowl. Cut margarine
or butter into small squares, add to the flour and
rub in with the tips of the fingers until the mixture
resembles fine breadcrumbs. Stir the sugar and
fruit into the mixture. Beat the eggs slightly with
the milk. Stir the mixture with a metal spoon.
Turn the mixture into the greased loaf tin and bake
on the middle shelf of the pre-heated oven for
1½ hours. Allow to stand in the tin for a few
minutes before turning on to a wire rack. This loaf
is delicious buttered or plain.
  Makes 1 1-pound loaf.

Sieve the dry ingredients into a bowl. Rub the fat
into the flour until the mixture resembles fine
breadcrumbs.
  Stir in the fruit and sugar. Add the egg and milk
and mix well. Turn the mixture into a 1-pound loaf
tin and bake as directed.

RAISIN BREAD

Baking time: 1 hour
  8 ounces (200 grams) self-raising flour
  1 teaspoon bicarbonate of soda
  1 ounce (25 grams) butter
  2 ounces (50 grams)
  ¼ pint (1½ decilitres) water (boiling)
  1 egg
  12 ounces (300 grams) raisins
  1 ounce (25 grams) chopped walnuts
    (optional)

Preheat the oven to 350°F, 180°C or Gas Mark 4.
Sieve all dry ingredients. Put sugar, butter and
raisins into a separate basin. Pour boiling water
over these and allow to cool. Stir in flour and egg.
Place in a small loaf tin and bake for 1 hour.
Makes 1 1-pound loaf.

GLAZED CHERRY BREAD

Baking time: 1 hour
  12 ounces (300 grams) self-raising flour
  ½ level teaspoon salt
  2 ounces (50 grams) caster sugar
  2 ounces (50 grams) walnuts, chopped
  2 ounces (50 grams) dates, stoned and
    chopped
  2 eggs
  2 rounded tablespoons malt extract
  ¼ pint (1 decilitre) milk
  2 ounces (50 grams) butter or margarine
GLAZE AND TOPPING:
  2 ounces (50 grams) caster sugar
  2 tablespoons water
  1 ounce (25 grams) walnuts
  1½ ounces (45 grams) glacé cherries

Preheat the oven to 325°F, 160°C or Gas Mark 3.
Grease 2 1-pound loaf tins well. Sieve flour and
salt into a bowl, add sugar, walnuts and dates.
Gently heat malt and butter or margarine until the
fat has melted. Pour into the centre of the flour
mixture with blended milk and eggs. Mix the
ingredients to a smooth, soft dough. Turn into 2
prepared loaf tins. Bake for 1 hour in a warm oven.
  To make the glaze: Heat sugar and water in a
pan and boil for 2–3 minutes until syrupy. When
the loaves are cooked, turn out onto a wire rack
and brush at once with glaze and decorate with
nuts and cherries.
Makes 2 1-pound loaves.

BANANA BREAD

Baking time: 1½ hours
- **10 ounces (250 grams) self-raising flour**
- **4 ounces (100 grams) butter or margarine**
- **6 ounces (150 grams) soft brown sugar**
- **3 eggs**
- **2 bananas**
- **1 level teaspoon cinnamon**
- **4(3) tablespoons milk**
- **4 ounces (100 grams) chopped apricots (optional)**
- **4 ounces (100 grams) chopped walnuts (optional)**

Preheat the oven to 325°F, 160°C or Gas Mark 3. Cream together the butter and sugar until soft and fluffy. Mash the bananas with a fork and beat into the creamed mixture. Add the eggs one by one with a little sieved flour if necessary. Add milk and fold in the sieved flour and cinnamon. If you wish to add apricots and walnuts, stir these in now. Bake in a moderate oven for 1½ hours, in a 2-pound loaf tin (less than 1 hour for 2 1-pound loaf tins). Delicious buttered as a tea-time treat.
Makes 1 2-pound loaf.

DATE AND WALNUT LOAF

Baking time: 1 hour
- **10 ounces (250 grams) plain flour**
- **½ teaspoon salt**
- **1 teaspoon mixed spice**
- **2 teaspoons cream of tartar**
- **1(½) egg**
- **6 ounces (150 grams) soft brown sugar**
- **½ large can evaporated milk**
- **1 teaspoon bicarbonate of soda**
- **2 ounces (50 grams) walnuts, chopped**
- **2 ounces (50 grams) stoned dates, chopped**

Preheat the oven to 375°F, 190°C or Gas Mark 5. Sieve together flour, salt, spice and cream of tartar. Beat egg, then add the sugar. Make evaporated milk up to ½ pint with water. Mix in bicarbonate of soda and mix into egg mixture. Stir in chopped walnuts and dates then stir in dry ingredients. Mix well and pour into prepared loaf tin (9 by 5 inches). Bake in a fairly hot oven, for about 1 hour. Turn out and cool on a wire rack. Serve sliced and buttered.
Makes 1 1-pound loaf.

CHEESE LOAF

Baking time: 40 minutes
- **8 ounces (200 grams) self-raising flour**
- **2 level teaspoons baking powder**
- **½ level teaspoon salt**
- **2 ounces (50 grams) margarine or butter**
- **3 tablespoons grated cheese**
- **¼ level teaspoon dry mustard**
- **¼ pint (1½ decilitres) milk**
- **1 egg**

Sieve the dry ingredients into a bowl and then rub the fat into the mixture until it resembles fine breadcrumbs. Add the grated cheese and then the milk and egg and mix with a round bladed knife to a soft dough. Knead and roll out the dough as for cheese scones (page 24).

Bake in a greased 1-pound loaf tin in a moderate oven, 350°F, 190°C or Gas Mark 5, for 40 minutes on the middle shelf. Delicious buttered for tea or toasted as base for savoury snacks.
Makes 1 1-pound cheese loaf.

SPICED NUT BREAD

Baking time: 1¼ hours
- **12 ounces (300 grams) plain flour**
- **1 teaspoon baking powder**
- **1 teaspoon salt**
- **¾ teaspoon nutmeg**
- **¾ teaspoon ginger**
- **2 eggs, beaten**
- **10 ounces (250 grams) soft brown sugar**

Set the oven to 350°F, 175°C, Gas Mark 4. Sieve together the dry ingredients, except the nuts. Beat the eggs in a large bowl and gradually blend in the brown sugar. Stir in the melted fat and the chopped nuts. Now add the flour mixture alternately with the milk until all the ingredients are well blended. Bake in a greased 1 pound loaf tin in a preheated moderate oven for about 1¼ hours until done. Allow to cool in the tin for about 10 minutes before turning out. Store in an airtight tin.
Makes 1 loaf.

BISCUITS

3

This is one aspect of family baking which can be a great economy as bought biscuits are very expensive and always seem to disappear very quickly. Extra biscuit mixture can be made and stored in a polythene bag in the refrigerator, then simply mix and bake as needed. Small children are always fascinated by animal shapes and the excess will give lots of fun to "the helpers". I find even the older ones love rolling out shapes . . . messy but marvellous for rainy afternoons!

Make a variety of biscuits on baking day.

BASIC BISCUIT MIXTURE

Baking time: 10–12 minutes
   4 ounces (100 grams) butter or margarine
   4 ounces (100 grams) caster sugar
   finely grated rind of 1 lemon
   8 ounces (200 grams) plain or
   self-raising flour
   ½ beaten egg

Preheat the oven to 375°F, 190°C or Gas Mark 5. Cream fat and sugar together until mixture is light and fluffy. Mix in the lemon rind. Beat in the egg and then gradually add the flour until a very firm mixture is obtained. Roll out the mixture to 1/8-inch thick and then cut into shapes or rounds as required. Bake in a moderate oven for 10–12 minutes.

Animal Biscuits

Makes about 30 biscuits.
Cut the shapes with animal cutters, bake as above then pipe eyes, nose and button with chocolate or icing.

Half and Half Biscuits

Dip half of the round biscuits into melted chocolate and allow to cool on oiled greaseproof paper.

Easter Biscuits

Add 2 ounces (50 grams) currants to the mixture before rolling out. Cut the biscuits with a 2-inch fluted cutter. Bake on a greased baking sheet for about 20 minutes at 350°F, 180°C or Gas Mark 4. Sprinkle with caster sugar while they are still hot. Makes 16 biscuits.

ALPHABET BISCUITS

Use the basic biscuit mixture (see above).
Roll out a quarter of an inch thick and cut out capital letters with a knife. You can make cardboard shapes of the letters but I think this is more trouble than making the biscuits. Bake in a moderate oven, 400°F, 200°C or Gas Mark 6, until the biscuits are golden brown. Allow the biscuits to cool, when they can be dipped in coloured glacé icing; or butter icing can be piped on as an outline for the letter.

SEMOLINA BISCUITS

Baking time: 20 minutes
   4 ounces (100 grams) butter or margarine
   4 ounces (100 grams) self-raising flour
   4 ounces (100 grams) semolina
   2 ounces (50 grams) caster sugar
   pinch of salt

Preheat the oven to 325°F, 160°C or Gas Mark 3. Cream the butter until soft in a bowl. Mix remaining ingredients together and add gradually to the butter. Knead into one piece. Roll out to about ¼-inch thick. Cut into rounds with a fluted cutter and bake for 15–20 minutes. Remove from the oven and sprinkle with caster sugar while still warm. Makes 16 biscuits.

COCONUT KISSES

Baking time: about 50 minutes
   2 egg whites
   4 ounces (100 grams) caster sugar
   3½ ounces (scant 100 grams) dessicated coconut

Preheat the oven to 275°F, 140°C or Gas Mark 1. Place the egg whites and sugar in a bowl over hot water and whisk until stiff, as in Italian meringues (see page 62). The water is unnecessary if you are using a mixer. Fold in the coconut. Drop in desertspoonfuls onto greased and floured baking sheets. Bake for about 50 minutes.
Makes 10 biscuits.

GROWING BISCUITS

Baking time: 15 minutes
   3 ounces (75 grams) butter or margarine
   3 ounces (75 grams) brown sugar
   1 egg yolk
   1 tablespoon golden syrup
   6 ounces (150 grams) self-raising flour
   2 ounces (50 grams) cornflour
   pinch of salt
   1 teaspoon ground ginger
   ¼ teaspoon bicarbonate soda

Preheat the oven to 400°F, 200°C or Gas Mark 6. Cream fat and sugar together until light and fluffy. Beat in egg yolk and syrup thoroughly. Work in sieved dry ingredients. Make into small balls, about the size of a walnut, with the hands and place on greased baking sheets. Allow the biscuits room to 'grow' or spread. Bake until they are spread and cracked, then finish off at 300°F, 150°C or Gas Mark 2.
Makes 48 biscuits.

GINGER NUTS (1)

Baking time: 15–18 minutes
- 4 ounces (100 grams) self-raising flour
- 1 desertspoon sugar
- 1 rounded teaspoon ginger
- 1 level teaspoon cinnamon
- ½ teaspoon bicarbonate of soda
- 2 ounces (50 grams) cooking fat
- 2 tablespoons sugar

Preheat the oven to 350°F, 170°C or Gas Mark 4. Sieve the dry ingredients into a bowl. Melt the fat and syrup together, cool a little then stir into the dry ingredients. Roll walnut-sized pieces in the hands and place well apart on baking sheets. Bake for 15–18 minutes.
Makes 14 biscuits.

GINGER NUTS (2)

Baking time: 20 minutes
- 4 ounces (100 grams) margarine
- 4 ounces (100 grams) sugar
- 2 tablespoons syrup
- 8 ounces (200 grams) self-raising flour
- 1 dessertspoon ground ginger
- 1 teaspoon baking soda

Preheat the oven to 325°F, 160°C or Gas Mark 3. Melt margarine, sugar and syrup in a pan. Add the dry ingredients and mix together. Roll the mixture in floured hands and make into small balls. Space them carefully on a greased baking sheet to allow spreading. Bake till brown in the oven.
Makes 30 biscuits.

MACAROONS

Baking time: 20–25 minutes
- 1 egg white
- ½ teaspoon orange flower water
- 2 ounces (50 grams) caster sugar
- 1 ounce (25 grams)
- 1 teaspoon ground rice

Preheat the oven to 300°F, 150°C or Gas Mark 2. Whisk the egg white until it is opaque, but not stiff. Add orange flower water and stir in dry ingredients. Form into small balls and place fairly well apart on rice paper on two baking sheets. Brush with beaten egg, and bake for 20–25 minutes. Remove rice papers from around the macaroons.
Makes 12 macaroons.

CRISPY LEMON BISCUITS

Baking time: 15 minutes
- 3 ounces (75 grams) butter
- 3 ounces (75 grams) caster sugar
- grated rind of 1 lemon
- 1 teaspoon lemon juice
- 6 ounces (150 grams) self-raising flour
- ¼ teaspoon salt
- 4 tablespoons evaporated milk
- glacé cherries
- caster sugar

Preheat the oven to 375°F, 190°C or Gas Mark 5. Cream butter and sugar. Stir in lemon rind and juice. Then gradually mix in flour, salt and evaporated milk. Form into walnut sized balls and place on greased baking sheet. Put half a glacé cherry in the centre of each biscuit. Sprinkle with caster sugar, bake in a fairly hot oven for about 15 minutes until lightly browned. Cool on a wire rack.
Makes 18 biscuits.

CHOCOLATE WALNUT COOKIES

Baking time: 20–30 minutes
- 5 ounces (125 grams) self-raising flour
- 1 ounce (25 grams) chocolate powder
- pinch salt
- 3 ounces (75 grams) butter
- 3 ounces (75 grams) caster sugar
- 2 ounces (50 grams) chopped walnuts
- 2 tablespoons evaporated milk

Preheat the oven to 350°F, 170°C or Gas Mark 4. Sieve together flour, chocolate powder and salt. Rub in butter, add sugar and walnuts. Bind with evaporated milk. Form into balls and place on a greased baking sheet. Bake in a moderate oven for 20–30 minutes until firm. Cool on a wire rack.
Makes 25 cookies.

FLORENTINES

Baking time: 15 minutes
- 4 ounces (100 grams) demerara sugar
- 4 ounces (100 grams) butter or margarine
- 4 ounces (100 grams) golden syrup
- 4 ounces (100 grams) plain flour
- 1½ ounces (45 grams) hazelnuts, chopped
- 1½ ounces (45 grams) blanched almonds, chopped
- ½ ounce (15 grams) angelica

COATING:
- 8 ounces (200 grams) plain chocolate

Preheat the oven to 325°F, 170°C or Gas Mark 3. Melt sugar, fat and syrup over a low heat (do not boil). Stir in the flour, nuts and angelica. Grease the baking sheets well and put a teaspoon of the mixture on for each biscuit. The mixture spreads so you will only manage 4–6 at a time, depending on the size of your baking sheet. Cook for 15 minutes in a preheated oven. Remove, allow to cool *slightly* and carefully remove the biscuits on to a wire tray with the aid of a flat-bladed knife. If the last one sticks, pop it back into the oven for a minute. Melt the chocolate over a bowl of hot water then coat the smooth side of the Florentines with chocolate. Store in an airtight tin and spoil yourself at coffee time!
Makes 30 Florentines.

ALMOND SWIRLS

Baking time: 15 minutes
- **4 ounces (100 grams) demerara sugar**
- **4 ounces (100 grams) butter or margarine**
- **4 ounces (100 grams) golden syrup**
- **4 ounces (100 grams) plain flour**
- **1½ ounces (45 grams) blanched almonds, chopped**

Make as for Florentines.
When almond swirls are removed from the oven allow to cool slightly then curl round the handle of a wooden spoon as for Brancy Snaps (see page 34).
Makes 24 biscuits.

CHEESE STRAWS

Baking time: 7–10 minutes
- **4 ounces (100 grams) plain flour**
- **pinch of salt**
- **pinch of cayenne pepper**
- **2 ounces (50 grams) margarine**
- **2 ounces (50 grams) grated cheese**
- **½ an egg yolk**
- **1-1½ teaspoon water**

Preheat the oven to 400°F, 200°C or Gas Mark 6. Sieve the dry ingredients into a bowl and rub in the margarine with the fingertips until the mixture is like fine breadcrumbs. Add egg yolk and water to the dry ingredients and make a stiff dough. Knead lightly with cool hands until the dough is free from cracks. Roll out and cut into straws with a sharp (not serrated) knife. Cut rings from the trimmings (I use a small plain cutter and the top of a large vegetable pipe but you can cut a circle out of the pastry with a knife). Place biscuits on a greased baking sheet and bake until golden brown.

Dip the ends in paprika pepper and put 6 straws in a ring. This mixture can be rolled out and cut into different shapes with plain or cocktail cutters if savouries are needed for a party.
Makes 48 straws.

GINGER BISCUIT MEN

Baking time: 15–20 minutes
- **4 ounces (100 grams) white cooking fat**
- **3(2) tablespoons syrup**
- **4 ounces (100 grams) sugar**
- **10 ounces (250 grams) flour**
- **3 teaspoons ground ginger**
- **1 teaspoon bicarbonate of soda**
- **glacé icing**
- **raisins**

Preheat the oven to 400°F, 200°C or Gas Mark 6. Slowly melt the fat, syrup and sugar over a low heat. Add the flour, ginger and bicarbonate of soda to make a stiff dough. Roll out to about a quarter of an inch thick and cut with a gingerbread man cutter. Prick well and bake on a greased baking sheet for 15–20 minutes in a moderate oven. When cool, ice the biscuits with glacé icing and use raisins as eyes, nose, buttons, etc. Smarties or chocolate buttons can be used as well.
Makes 12 biscuits.

BROWNIES

Baking time: 30 minutes
- **7 ounces (175 grams) caster sugar**
- **1½ ounces (50 grams) butter**
- **1 egg**
- **1 teaspoon vanilla essence**
- **2 ounces (50 grams) plain chocolate**
- **4 ounces (100 grams) self-raising flour**
- **1 small can evaporated milk**
- **2 ounces (50 grams) chopped walnuts**
- **glacé cherries and walnuts**

Preheat the oven to 350°F, 180°C or Gas Mark 4. Beat sugar, butter, egg and vanilla essence together until light and fluffy. Melt chocolate in a basin over hot water and add to the sugar mixture. Stir sieved flour into sugar mixture alternately with evaporated milk. Stir in chopped walnuts. Mix well and pour into a greased 9-inch square tin or roasting tin. Bake in a moderate oven for about 30 minutes. Turn out and cool on wire rack. Ice with fudge or mocha icing. Cut into squares. Decorate with glacé cherries and walnuts.
Makes about 12 brownies.

BRANDY SNAPS

Baking time: 10 minutes
scant 2 ounces (50 grams) flour
½ level teaspoon ground ginger
2 ounces (50 grams) butter
2 ounces (50 grams) sugar
2(1½) tablespoons golden syrup

Preheat the oven to 325°F, 170°C or Gas Mark 3. Sieve the flour and ginger together in a small bowl. Slowly melt the butter, syrup and sugar in a saucepan. When melted and well mixed, add the flour and stir well. Thoroughly grease a baking sheet (the non-stick variety is ideal). Drop on a teaspoonful for each snap and allow at least 3 inches for each to spread. It is best to cook just one tray at a time since you have to roll the biscuits as they are cooling. Bake in the middle of the oven for about 10 minutes until they are golden brown. Remove from the oven and allow to cool for 2–3 minutes. After loosening the biscuits with a palette knife, press and form them round the greased handle of a wooden spoon and allow to cool. Eat as crunchy biscuits or fill with fresh whipped cream before serving.
Makes 16 snaps.

SCOTTISH SHORTBREAD

Baking time: 40–60 minutes depending on the thickness.
This recipe always conjures up childhood pictures of Hogmanay (New Year's Eve) in Scotland. The delicious buttery smell of the shortbread and the agony of having to wait until after the magic hour of midnight to taste some.
8 ounces (200 grams) superfine flour
4 ounces (100 grams) rice flour
8 ounces (200 grams) butter
4 ounces (100 grams) caster sugar

Preheat the oven to 375°F, 190°C or Gas Mark 5. Sieve the 2 flours several times and put in the warming drawer of the cooker for a few minutes to make sure that it is absolutely dry. Now sieve the flour on to the table. Mix the butter and sugar together by hand on another part of the table. Gradually work in the flours to the fat and sugar mixture with the hands, keeping the cake all together. Now press the dough into two cakes with the hands about ¾-inch thick and about 8 inches in diameter. Pinch the edges neatly with the finger and thumb then prick all over with a fork. I have recently treated myself to a wooden shortbread mould from Elizabeth David's shop. I brush it over with oil and flour it well and it produces rather neat little cakes which are easy to store. Put into a fairly hot oven for about 20 minutes then turn down to 325°F, 160°C or Gas Mark 3 for the remaining time until it is pale golden.
Makes 2 8-inch cakes.

Brandy Snaps filled with whipped cream.
Scottish Shortbread.

OATMEAL CRUNCHIES

Baking time: 10 minutes
- **4 ounces (100 grams) plain flour**
- **1 (1¼) teaspoons bicarbonate of soda**
- **¼ teaspoon salt**
- **3 ounces (75 grams) rolled oats**
- **2 ounces (50 grams) desiccated coconut**
- **2 ounces (50 grams) butter**
- **4 ounces (100 grams) caster sugar**
- **2 tablespoons golden syrup**
- **3 (2½) tablespoons evaporated milk**

Preheat the oven to 375°F, 190°C or Gas Mark 5. Mix dry ingredients together. Cream butter, sugar and syrup. Stir in dry ingredients alternately with evaporated milk. Roll into walnut-sized balls and place (about 2 inches apart) on a greased baking sheet. Bake in a fairly hot oven for about 10 minutes until lightly browned. Cool on wire rack. Makes 16 crunchies.

Oatmeal Crunchies

Walnut Brownies

WALNUT BROWNIES

Baking time: 25 minutes
- **4 ounces (125 grams) plain flour**
- **½ level teaspoon baking powder**
- **4 ounces (125 grams) margarine**
- **2 ounces (50 grams) cocoa powder**
- **1 teaspoon vanilla essence**
- **3 eggs**
- **8 ounces (225 grams) caster sugar**
- **4 ounces (125 grams) walnuts**

Preheat the oven to 350°F, 180°C or Gas Mark 4. Sieve the flour and baking powder. Melt the fat and gradually add the cocoa to the fat until it is blended. Remove from the heat and stir in the vanilla essence. Allow to cool. Line a 10 by 6 inch tin with greaseproof paper. Whisk the eggs and sugar together for a few minutes then add the cooled cocoa mixture. Fold in the sieved flour and walnuts. Bake for 25 minutes, remove from the oven, allow to cool slightly, then cut into squares. If required, decorate with a piece of walnut.

For 2-tone brownies omit the cocoa powder from half the mixture. Use only 1 egg to mix. Put plain mixture at the bottom of the tin and chocolate on top.
Makes 32 brownies.

CAKES

There are several methods of making cakes but certain points should always be kept in mind. A little organisation goes a long way towards successful cake making.

Points to bear in mind are:

1. Read the recipe thoroughly.

2. Check to see that you have all the ingredients you need.
3. Prepare the cake tin first.
4. Turn the oven to the required temperature. Oven heat is important in cake making and, as a general rule, the richer the cake the cooler the oven.

Plain Cakes

These are more economical and easier to make than rich fruit cakes.

Plain cakes are made by rubbing the fat into the flour. The butter or margarine used is a half of the weight of the flour or less. Fruit or nuts can be added. They look rather homely with slight cracking on a dome-shaped top. The texture should be even, with not too many holes and no doughy patches.

They are best eaten within 3–4 days.

TO PREPARE A CAKE TIN:
1. Use double greaseproof paper.
2. Cut out a shape to fit the bottom of the tin.
3. Cut out a long strip of greaseproof paper and fold it double to fit inside the tin, allowing an extra 2 inches on the circumference and an extra 2 inches on the depth.
4. Make a 1-inch hem along the folded edge.
5. Cut into the hem at an angle at ½-inch intervals. You now have a serrated edge.
6. Brush the paper for the bottom and sides with melted oil or fat.
7. Fit the paper for the sides of the tin into the tin with the serrated edge downwards.
8. Now put the paper for the bottom into the tin so that it rests on the serrated edge.
Note: Make sure that your paper fits snugly, otherwise the shape of your cake will suffer.

COCONUT CAKE

Baking time: 1 hour
8 ounces (225 grams) plain flour
pinch of salt
1 teaspoon baking powder
5 ounces (150 grams) margarine
2 ounces (50 grams) coconut

4 ounces (125 grams) caster sugar
2 eggs
4 tablespoons milk
1 teaspoon desiccated coconut for the top

Preheat the oven to 350°F, 180°C or Gas Mark 4. Sieve the flour, salt and baking powder. Cut the fat into small pieces and rub in with the tips of the fingers until the mixture resembles fine breadcrumbs. Add coconut and sugar. Make a well in the centre and add the eggs and milk. Mix to a dropping consistency. Put the mixture into the prepared 6-inch cake tin, sprinkle with coconut and bake in a moderate oven for 1–1¼ hours. Makes 1 6-inch cake.

Variations

EVERYDAY FRUIT CAKE: Use 4–6 ounces (125–175 grams) mixed dried fruit in place of the sultanas.
SEED CAKE: Omit the fruit and stir in 2 teaspoons caraway seeds and a few drops of vanilla essence.

COMMON FAULTS IN SANDWICH CAKES
1. A domed top:
   too little raising agent
   oven temperature too high.
2. A hollow top:
   too much raising agent.
3. A very pale cake:
   the oven is too cool
   the cake has been cooked on too low a shelf.
4. The cake is speckled:
   the fat and sugar have not been creamed sufficiently
   granulated sugar may have been used.
5. Doughy inside:
   oven too hot
   cake baked too high in the oven.

VICTORIA SANDWICH CAKE

Baking time: 40 minutes

- 6 ounces (175 grams) butter or margarine
- 6 ounces (175 grams) caster sugar
- 3 large eggs
- 6 ounces (175 grams) self-raising flour
- pinch of salt
- 1 tablespoon boiling water

Preheat the oven to 350°F, 180°C or Gas Mark 4. See method illustrated below.

Variations on Victoria Sandwich Cake

LEMON OR ORANGE CAKE: To the Victoria Sandwich mixture add the grated rind of 1 lemon or 1 orange when creaming. Add 1 tablespoon lemon or orange juice to the butter icing (see page 58) and also to the glacé icing. Decorate the top with lemon or orange sugared slices.

RASPBERRY OR STRAWBERRY CAKE: Make a Victoria Sandwich and fill the cake with whipped cream and fresh or tinned fruit. Decorate the top with fruit and cream or sprinkle with icing sugar.

WALNUT LAYER CAKE: Add 1 ounce chopped walnuts to the basic mixture and decorate the top of the cake with coffee glacé icing and halved walnuts.

MOCHA CAKE: Blend 1 tablespoon of cocoa with 2 tablespoons of boiling water and 1 dessertspoon coffee essence. Add this to the Victoria Sandwich basic creamed mixture before adding the eggs. This cake is particularly rich and delicious if the top and sides are coated with Mocha butter icing (see page 58) and the cake is then rolled in chopped walnuts, flaked chocolate, or crushed cereal. Finish the top with chocolate buttons. To coat the cake use 12 ounces (350 grams) icing sugar.

Step 1. Cream the fat and sugar together until the mixture is light and fluffy. Sieve the flour and salt. Add the eggs one by one beating thoroughly. Add a little sieved flour with the second and third egg.

Step 2. Add the sieved flour and salt and fold in with a sharp-edged metal spoon until all the flour is absorbed.

Step 3. Divide the mixture into the prepared tins. If you are using non-stick tins it is not necessary to line the tins with paper. Bake in a moderate oven, 350°F, 180°C or Gas Mark 4, for 20 minutes. To test the cake, press lightly with the finger tips and the cake should spring back leaving no impression.

Step 4. Allow the cakes to cool then sandwich together with jam and sprinkle with caster or icing sugar.

QUICK VICTORIA SANDWICH

Baking time: 25–30 minutes
   4 ounces (100 grams) self-raising flour
   1 level teaspoon baking powder
   4 ounces (100 grams) caster sugar
   2 large (medium) eggs
   4 ounces (100 grams) soft margarine

Preheat the oven to 325°F, 170°C or Gas Mark 3. Sieve the flour and baking powder in a bowl. Add sugar, stir and then break in 2 eggs and the margarine. Beat ingredients together with a wooden spoon for 2–3 minutes. Put the mixture into lined and greased 7-inch sandwich cake tins and bake for 25–30 minutes on the middle shelf. Sandwich with jam or icing.

Note: There are many soft margarines available now which make excellent "throw everything in" cakes.

RICH CHOCOLATE CAKE

Baking time: 1½–1¾ hours
   5 ounces (150 grams) butter or margarine
   5 ounces (150 grams) caster sugar
   4 eggs
   4 ounces (100 grams) plain chocolate
   1 level teaspoon cocoa
   3 tablespoons warm water
   6 ounces (175 grams) self-raising flour

Preheat the oven to 325°F, 170°C or Gas Mark 3. Grease a 7-inch cake tin and line the bottom. Cream together the margarine and sugar. Melt the chocolate over a pan of hot water, add to the creamed mixture. Mix the cocoa with the warm water and add to the creamed mixture. Separate the eggs. Add the yolks to the mixture and beat well. Fold in the sieved flour. Beat the whites until stiff and fold in carefully. Pour mixture into the prepared tin and bake for 1½–1¾ hours.

When the cake is cool cut it into three layers. Sandwich the layers with chocolate butter icing. Decorate the outside of the cake with butter icing or coating chocolate, finish with chocolate squares, flaked chocolate, walnuts or almonds.

STRAWBERRY FLAN

Baking time: 30 minutes
   1 sponge flan
   8 ounces (200 grams) strawberries
   redcurrant jelly

Make a Victoria Sandwich using 4 ounces each of fat, flour and sugar and 2 eggs. Bake in a greased sponge flan tin for 25–30 minutes in a moderate oven, 350°F, 180°C or Gas Mark 4. Arrange the hulled strawberries in the cooled flan. Heat the redcurrant jelly and pour over the strawberries to glaze.

Sponge Flan being filled with strawberries.

PEPPERMINT CHOCOLATE LAYER CAKE

Baking time: 1¼ hours

   6 ounces (175 grams) margarine
   6 ounces (175 grams) caster sugar
   1 rounded teaspoon cocoa
   2 tablespoons warm water
   3 eggs
   8 ounces (225 grams) self-raising flour
   1 teaspoon baking powder
PEPPERMINT BUTTER ICING:
   12 ounces (325 grams) icing sugar
   3 ounces (100 grams) butter or margarine
   few drops of peppermint extract
   few drops of green colouring
   3 tablespoons milk
TO DECORATE:
   chocolate flake

Prepare a 6-inch round or square tin by greasing and lining as desribed on page 36. Preheat the oven to 350°F, 180°C or Gas Mark 4. Cream the fat and sugar together until the mixture is light and fluffy. Add the cocoa powder which has been blended with the water and beat thoroughly. Add the eggs one by one with a little of the sieved flour with the last two eggs. Sieve the flour and baking powder onto the creamed mixture and fold in with a metal spoon. Turn the mixture into the prepared tin and bake in a moderate oven for 1¼ hours. Allow to cool slightly, turn on to a wire tray and remove the paper. When the cake is thoroughly cooled, split into three and sandwich together with peppermint butter icing (see page 58 for method). Finish by either spreading or piping the top with butter icing and decorating with chocolate flake or grated plain chocolate if desired.

Marble Cake

A slice of Peppermint Chocolate Cake.

MARBLE CAKE

Baking time: 50 minutes

   6 ounces (175 grams) caster sugar
   6 ounces (175 grams) margarine
   3 eggs
   6 ounces (175 grams) self-raising flour
   1 tablespoon cocoa powder
   2 tablespoons water

Grease a 1-pound loaf tin and preheat the oven to 325°F, 170°C or Gas Mark 3.

Cream the fat and sugar until light and fluffy. Add the eggs with a little of the sieved flour added with the second and third eggs. Fold in the flour with a metal spoon and divide the mixture into two parts. Blend the cocoa with the water and add to one part of the mixture. Alternatively use a few drops of colouring in place of the chocolate. Put alternate spoons of cholate and plain mixture into loaf tin and run a fork lengthwise through the mixture. Bake got 50 minutes in the centre of a moderate oven.

EASTER DAY GATEAU

Baking time: 1¼ hours
  6 ounces (175 grams) butter
  6 ounces (175 grams) caster sugar
  grated rind and juice of an orange
  3 eggs
  6 ounces (175 grams) self-raising flour
  1 ounce (25 grams) almonds
FILLING AND TOPPING:
  ½ pint (3 decilitres) double cream
  1 ounce (25 grams) caster sugar
  1 tablespoon apricot jam, sieved
  8 slices of fresh orange or
    8 marzipan "oranges"
  2 ounces (50 grams) toasted almonds

Preheat the oven to 350°F, 180°C or Gas Mark 4. Grease and line a 7-inch square cake tin. Cream butter, sugar, orange rind and juice together until light and fluffy. Blend eggs and add a little at a time, beating well after each addition. Skin and finely chop the almonds. Fold flour and chopped nuts into creamed mixture. Turn into prepared tin and bake for about 1¼ hours.
To prepare almonds: Blanch shelled almonds in boiling water and slip off skin. With point of a small knife separate halves, and slowly brown under the grill.
To make marzipan oranges: Colour 4 ounces almond paste with 2 drops of orange colouring. Divide into 8 and mould into balls. Lightly mark with a knife to represent orange skin. Stick a clove into top of ball and make leaves of angelica.
  Allow cake to cool and then split in half. Whip cream with sugar. Put a third of the cream between layers of cake. Spread the rest on top of cake and around the sides. Decorate top of cake with a circle of marzipan oranges or fresh skinned orange segments. Thickly cover sides of cake with browned almonds.

MADEIRA CAKE

Baking time: 1¼ hours
  5 ounces (150 grams) butter
  5 ounces (150 grams) caster sugar
  grated rind of 1 lemon
  3 large eggs
  8 ounces (225 grams) plain flour
  2 level teaspoons baking powder
  1½ tablespoons milk
  1 slice citron peel

Preheat the oven to 350°F, 180°C or Gas Mark 4. Cream the fat and sugar together until light and

fluffy. Beat in the eggs one by one. Fold in the sieved dry ingredients. Turn the mixture into a greased 7-inch cake tin. Bake in a moderate oven for 1¼ hours. After the cake has been in the oven for 20 minutes, place the citron peel on top, without removing the cake from the oven.
Makes 1 7-inch cake.

CANADIAN COCONUT SPONGE

  3 ounces (100 grams) margarine
  4 ounces (125 grams) caster sugar
  2 egg yolks (large)
  4 ounces (125 grams) self-raising flour
  drop of milk
TOPPING:
  2 egg whites
  scant 2 ounces (50 grams) caster sugar
  2 ounces (50 grams) coconut

Preheat the oven to 325°F, 160°C or Gas Mark 3. Cream the margarine and sugar together, add the two egg yolks and beat. Add the flour and mix to a dropping consistency with a little milk. Turn into a 10 by 6 inch baking tin. Whisk the two egg whites until stiff, add sugar and coconut. Pile on top of mixture and bake for 1 hour.

BUTTERFLY CAKES

Baking time: 10–12 minutes
  4 ounces (125 grams) self-raising flour
  3 ounces (100 grams) margarine
  3 ounces (100 grams) caster sugar
  2 (large) eggs
  1 tablespoon milk
  whipped cream or butter icing
  jam
  icing sugar

Preheat the oven to 375°F, 190°C or Gas Mark 5. Beat the fat until soft, add sugar and cream together until light and fluffy. Sieve the flour, add the eggs one at a time with a tablespoon of flour, beating well after each addition. Stir in milk and more flour, beat again, add remaining flour and cut in to the mixture but do not beat.
  Grease and flour 12 patty tins, or use paper cases, half fill with the mixture. Bake for 10–12 minutes near the top of the oven until firm, well risen and golden brown. Allow to cool. Cut off the tops and then cut them into two halves to look like butterfly wings. Spread with jam, pipe or pile cream on to the cake then arrange the wings on top and dust with sieved icing sugar.

RICH CAKES

These are cakes where the amount of margarine or butter used is more than half the weight of the flour. Richer types of cakes are usually made by the creaming method. The volume and texture of the cake depends on the thorough creaming of the fat and sugar, to introduce as much air as possible. The air which has been beaten in expands, helping the cake to rise with an even texture. Less raising agent is needed as a result of all this beaten-in air, therefore plain flour can be used in most rich fruit cake recipes.

TO MAKE A SUCCESSFUL CREAMED CAKE

1 Creaming: Make sure fat and sugar are creamed thoroughly. Mixture should be soft and fluffy and if butter or margarine is used the colour will lighten to almost white as creaming progresses.
2. Eggs: Add each egg separately. Beat into the mixture to add more air to the cake. The mixture should be thick and creamy looking with no traces of egg left before the next one is added.

To avoid curdling, add a little sieved flour with the second egg and each one after.
3. Folding in dry ingredients: Do not beat flour into the cake mixture but fold it in with a sharp edged metal spoon. Beating with a wooden spoon will cause loss of air which has already been creamed into the mixture.

TO BAKE A RICH CAKE
The middle shelf is most suitable for rich cakes as the temperature is low for a long baking time. To protect rich fruit cakes from becoming hard on the outside, tie a double strip of brown paper round the outside of the tin and place the tin on a double sheet of brown paper. A piece of greaseproof should be placed on top of the cake for the last 1½ hours.

APPEARANCE
A rich fruit cake should have a flat top with no cracks. When cut, the fruit should be evenly distributed throughout the cake. There should be no soggy patches inside.

TRADITIONAL FRUIT CAKE

Baking time: 3–4 hours
> **6 ounces (175 grams) butter**
> **6 ounces (175 grams) caster sugar**
> **4 eggs**
> **6 ounces (175 grams) currants**
> **4 ounces (125 grams) sultanas**
> **3 ounces (75 grams) raisins**
> **2 ounces (50 grams) chopped peel**
> **1 ounce (25 grams) cherries**
> **rind of 1 lemon**
> **4 ounces (125 grams) self-raising flour**
> **4 ounces (125 grams) plain flour**
> **pinch of salt**
> **½ teaspoon nutmeg**
> **½ teaspoon cinnamon**

Preheat the oven to 300°F, 150°C or Gas Mark 2. Cream fat and sugar together until light and fluffy. Beat eggs into the mixture one by one (add a little flour with the last two, if necessary). Sieve in the flour and fold in with a metal spoon. Fold in the fruit and turn into a lined 8-inch cake tin. Tie a band of brown paper outside the cake tin and stand on a piece of brown paper in the oven. Bake for about 3–4 hours in a low oven.

Decorate with Almond Paste (see page 60) and Royal Icing (see page 60) or Fondant (see page 61).

FAMILY FRUIT CAKE

Baking time: 5 hours
> **8 ounces (200 grams) margarine**
> **4 ounces (100 grams) soft brown sugar**
> **4 (3) level tablespoons golden syrup**
> **grated rind of 2 lemons**
> **4 eggs**
> **2 ounces (50 grams) ground almonds**
> **1 tablespoon sherry**
> **8 ounces (200 grams) plain flour**
> **pinch of salt**
> **2–3 pounds (1–1½ kilograms)**
> **mixed fruit**
> **4 ounces (100 grams) mixed peel**
> **or cherries**
> **2 teaspoons mixed spice**
> **freshly grated nutmeg**

Preheat the oven to 300°F, 150°C or Gas Mark 2. Line and grease a 9-inch round or square tin. Cream margarine and sugar together until light and fluffy. Add lemon rind. Sieve flour, salt and spice together. Beat in eggs one at a time, together with a little flour with the last two eggs. Add ground almonds and fold in fruit, flour and sherry. Spread into the tin and make a hollow in the centre. Tie a double piece of brown paper round the sides of tin and sit the cake on a double sheet of brown paper. Bake in the middle shelf of a cool oven for 1 hour. Reduce the heat to 275°F, 130°C or Gas Mark 1 and cook for a further 4 hours or until a skewer comes out clean. Allow to cool then turn out on to a wire tray. The cake will keep for weeks in an airtight tin and it becomes more delicious the longer it is kept!

A delicious Fruit Cake cooling on wire tray.

COMMON FAULTS IN FRUIT CAKES

1. If the cake is too dry:
   not enough liquid
   not enough fat or sugar
   over-baking
   too much raising agent.

2. If the cake has a hard crusty outside and has a damp uncooked patch in the centre:
   the oven is too hot
   too much liquid e.g. gingerbread mixture when there is syrup in the recipe.
3. If the cake sinks in the middle:
   too much raising agent has been used in rich cake
   the mixture may not have been creamed enough.
4. If the fruit sinks to the bottom of the cake:
   cake mixture may have had too much liquid added
   there may be too much raising agent.
5. Cracked fruit cakes are caused by:
   the oven being too hot
   the tin being too small.
6. Bad texture can be caused by:
   too much raising agent (can produce holes)
   badly mixed flour
   not enough raising agent or enough liquid (close texture)
   curdling during mixing.

Football Cake

Baking time: 2½ hours

1 cake mixture (see traditional fruit cake, page 41) cooked in 2 greased pudding basins
1 cake board covered with butter icing (see page 58) coloured for the appropriate team
12 ounces (350 grams) almond paste (1½ times the recipe for Simnel cake recipe, page 60), with 2 tablespoons cocoa added to the icing sugar before you make the paste
apricot jam, warmed and sieved
Royal Icing (see page 60, but use 1 egg white instead of 3)

Cut a piece from one side of each cake so that the football will stand up. Sandwich cakes together by brushing the tops with apricot jam and then using a thin piece of almond paste the same size as the surfaces. Leave to firm for a while. Roll out the almond paste and brush the cake all over with apricot jam. Cover the cake, smoothing with your hands. Put on the covered board and mark the seams of the ball with a pastry wheel. Pipe the boy's name and age on the side. Pipe an outline of the lacing at the top of the ball. Pipe round the bottom of the cake to cover the join between the cake and the board. Put candles at each end like goal posts.

DUNDEE CAKE

Baking time: 2¼ hours

6 ounces (175 grams) butter
6 ounces (175 grams) soft brown sugar
3 eggs
1 tablespoon milk
4 ounces (125 grams) plain flour
4 ounces (100 grams) self-raising flour
1 teaspoon mixed spice
5 ounces (150 grams) sultanas
1 ounce (25 grams) currants
1 ounce (25 grams) glacé cherries
2 ounces (50 grams) blanched, halved almonds

Preheat the oven to 350°F, 180°C or Gas Mark 4. Prepare and line a 7-inch cake tin (see page 36). Cream the butter and sugar together until light and fluffy. Add the eggs one by one with a tablespoon of the measured flour with the second and third eggs. Then add the milk. Now sieve the flour salt and mixed spice together. Add half the flour to the mixture then stir in the fruit and the remaining flour. Put the mixture into the prepared tin and arrange the halved almonds on top. Put the cake into the preheated oven for 1 hour then cover with a piece of greaseproof paper and turn the oven down to 300°F, 160°C or Gas Mark 2 for 1¼ hours.

CHERRY CAKE

Baking time: 1¼ hours

7 ounces (200 grams) self-raising flour
pinch of salt
6 ounces (175 grams) glacé cherries
4 ounces (125 grams) butter
4 ounces (125 grams) caster sugar
3 eggs
1 ounce (25 grams) ground almonds

Preheat the oven to 350°F, 180°C or Gas Mark 4. Prepare and line a 6-inch tin. Sieve the flour and salt. Wash the cherries and dry with kitchen paper. Toss in a little of the sieved flour. Cream the butter and sugar together until the mixture is light and fluffy. Beat in the eggs one at a time with a spoonful of flour with the second and third eggs. Fold in with a metal spoon the ground almonds, cherries and remainder of the flour. Put the mixture in the prepared tin and bake in a moderate oven for 1¼ hours on the middle shelf.

Simnel Cake

SIMNEL CAKE

Baking time: 2¾ hours

   6 ounces (175 grams) butter or margarine
   6 ounces (175 grams) caster sugar
   4 eggs
   8 ounces (225 grams) plain flour
   ½ teaspoon salt
   1 teaspoon baking powder
   1 teaspoon mixed spice
   1 teaspoon cinnamon
   12 ounces (325 grams) mixed fruit,
      washed
   2 ounces (50 grams) candied peel,
      chopped
   juice and rind of 1 lemon

ALMOND PASTE:

   8 ounces (225 grams) ground almonds
   6 ounces (175 grams) caster sugar
   4 ounces (100 grams) icing sugar, sieved
   2 egg yolks
   juice of 1 lemon
   Easter chickens, for decoration

Preheat the oven to 350°F, 180°C or Gas Mark 4. Make up almond paste first. Mix the sugar and ground almonds together. Make a well in the centre and add egg yolks and lemon juice. Mix with a small palette knife or fork and knead to a smooth paste. Cut a greaseproof paper pattern slightly smaller than the bottom of the prepared 7-inch square or 8-inch round tin, and roll out one-third of the paste to fit this. Put the remaining paste, wrapped up, in the refrigerator. Remember to take it out to return to room temperature before using.

Cream sugar and fat until light and fluffy. Sieve flour, salt and spices together. Beat in the eggs one at a time, using a little of the sieved flour with the last two eggs. Fold in the remaining sieved flour, fruit and lemon juice. Turn half of the cake mixture into the greased tin, and place the almond paste shape on top. Tap the tin to level out mixture and then add the remaining cake mixture. Level out and hollow slightly in the middle. Put the cake in the centre of a moderate oven for 40 minutes; lower heat to 325°F, 170°C or Gas Mark 3 and bake for a further 2 hours. Allow to cool. To finish cake: Divide the remaining paste into two. If the top of the cake is not absolutely level, patch it with a little almond paste. Roll out one piece of the paste to the size of the top of the cake. Use caster sugar for rolling out. Brush the top of the cake with hot sieved apricot jam and turn onto the paste. Turn upright and pinch up the edge of the marzipan.

Roll the remaining paste into the shape of eggs; glaze these and the cake with egg and brown under the grill.

Arrange the egg shapes with chickens on top of the cake and tie a yellow satin ribbon round the middle.

GINGERBREAD AND FRUIT CAKES

So far I have dealt with the rubbing-in and the creaming methods of making cakes. Now I am going to deal with cakes which are made by heating or boiling the sugar, fat and treacle ingredients. Various raising agents may be used. The texture of this type of cake is damp and close and improves with keeping. Gingerbreads and some fruit cakes can be made by this method.

GINGERBREAD

Baking time: 1¼–1½ hours

12 ounces (350 grams) plain flour
3 ounces (100 grams) sugar
1½ teaspoons mixed spice
1½ level teaspoons bicarbonate of soda
3 teaspoons ground ginger
6 ounces (175 grams) lard or butter
9 ounces (250 grams) black treacle
3 ounces (75 grams) golden syrup
12 tablespoons milk
3 eggs

Preheat the oven to 325°F, 170°C or Gas Mark 3. Grease an 8 to 9-inch cake tin and line the bottom with greaseproof paper.

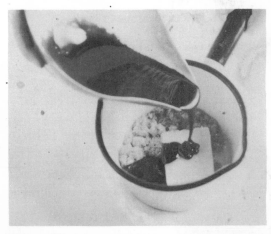

Step 1. Put the lard or butter, black treacle and golden syrup into a saucepan and heat until the fat has melted. Allow to cool.

This makes a delicious children's tea-time treat served with a crisp apple.

Step 2. Sieve the dry ingredients into a mixing bowl. Warm the milk in the same saucepan to make sure that the treacle mixture is not wasted. Add the fat and treacle mixture to the dry ingredients and beat thoroughly. Lastly add the egg to the mixture.

Step 3. Pour the gingerbread mixture into the prepared tin and cook in the preheated oven for 1¼ hours.

Step 4. Test the cake carefully with a skewer then remove from the oven and allow to cool in the tin for 10 minutes before turning out on to a wire tray. To mature, store in an airtight tin for a few days before using.

VALENTINE GINGER UPSIDE-DOWN-CAKE

Baking time: 1 hour
TOPPING:
    ½ ounce (15 grams) butter
    1 dessertspoon honey
    2 pears, peeled, cored and halved
    a few maraschino cherries
    a few angelica leaves
FOR THE CAKE:
    12 ounces (325 grams) plain flour
    ½ teaspoon bicarbonate of soda
    1½ teaspoons ground ginger
    pinch of mixed spice
    pinch of ground cinnamon
    8 ounces (200 grams) syrup or
        6 ounces (150 grams) syrup and
    2 ounces (50 grams) black treacle
    2 ounces (50 grams) butter
    4 ounces (100 grams) brown sugar
    2 small eggs, well beaten
    4 tablespoons milk
    a little heated apricot jam

Preheat the oven to 350°F, 180°C or Gas Mark 3.
Grease a heart-shaped tin with the butter. Pour
the honey on the base. Place the cherries in the
centre of three pear halves and place them flat
side down on the base of the tin.
Sieve the flour, bicarbonate of soda and the spices
into a bowl. Make a well in the centre. Put the
treacle, butter and sugar into a saucepan. Heat
gently until butter has melted. Pour into the flour
mixture then add beaten eggs and milk and beat
well. Turn into tin and bake for about 1 hour or
until firm to the touch. Turn upside down onto a
serving dish and glaze with sieved apricot jam.
Decorate with the remaining cherries and a few
angelica leaves.
Makes 6 servings.

FRUIT CAKE

Baking time: 1¼ hours
    8 ounces (200 grams) self-raising flour
    pinch of salt
    ½ teaspoon grated nutmeg
    1 teaspoon mixed spice
    4 ounces (100 grams) butter or margarine
    4 ounces (100 grams) sultanas
    2 ounces (50 grams) currants
    13 (12) tablespoons hot water
    ½ level teaspoon bicarbonate of soda

Prepare a 6-inch cake tin (see page 36).
Preheat the oven to 350°F, 180°C or Gas Mark 4.
Sieve the flour, spices and salt together in a mixing
bowl. Place the butter, sugar, fruit and water in a
saucepan and stir over a low heat until the fat is
melted and the sugar is completely dissolved.
Allow the mixture to come up to the boil then
lower the heat and simmer for 2–3 minutes. Allow
to cool until just lukewarm. Add the bicarbonate
of soda to the cooled mixture and stir in quickly.
Pour the liquid into the centre of the flour and mix
thoroughly. Turn into the prepared tin and bake on
the middle shelf of a moderate over for 1¼ hours.
Allow the cake to stand for a few minutes before
turning out of the tin and cooling on a wire tray.

FRUIT GINGERBREAD

Cooking time: 1¼ hours
    8 ounces (200 grams) plain flour
    4 ounces (100 grams) butter
    8 ounces (200 grams) black treacle
    ¼ pint (scant 1½ decilitres) milk
    2 eggs
    2 ounces (50 grams) sugar
    1 teaspoon mixed spice
    2 teaspoons ground ginger
    ½ teaspoon bicarbonate of soda
    2 ounces (50 grams) sultanas
    1 ounce (25 grams) glacé cherries,
        halved
    1 ounce (25 grams) crystallised ginger,
        chopped

Preheat the oven to 325°F, 170°C or Gas Mark 3.
Grease a square 7-inch cake tin and line it with
greaseproof paper. Warm the butter, treacle, sugar
and milk all together in a large saucepan. Allow to
cool. Blend in the beaten eggs. Add the cooled
mixture to the sieved dry ingredients. Add the
fruit. Turn the mixture into the prepared tin. Bake
slightly below the middle of a slow oven for about
1¼ hours.

Gingerbread with
Crystallised Ginger on top.

WHISKED SPONGES

A whisked sponge is the lightest of cakes. The texture depends on the air beaten in with the eggs and sugar, as only a small proportion of flour is added. For good results, follow the recipes to the letter and weigh the ingredients carefully. Also take note of the points on the opposite page.

This is a soft cake which keeps well and is suitable for filling with whipped cream. Dust with sieved icing sugar.

SPONGE CAKE

Baking time: 20–25 minutes
- **3 eggs**
- **4½ ounces (125 grams) caster sugar**
- **3 ounces (85 grams) plain flour**
- **pinch of salt**

Preheat the oven to 375°F, 190°C or Gas Mark 5. Prepare an 8-inch cake tin by brushing with oil or fat. Sprinkle with caster sugar and shake off surplus. Put a little flour in the tin and shake well round. Empty out any surplus flour. Sieve the flour and salt several times.

Step 1. Place a bowl on top of a large saucepan of boiling water. Put the eggs in the bowl and gradually add the sugar, beating all the time, until the mixture is thick and creamy. When the mixture streams solidly off the whisk it is ready.

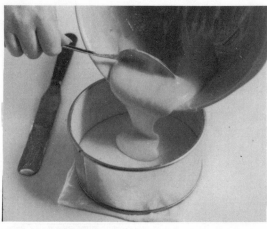

Step 3. Turn into the prepared tin immediately and bake in the preheated oven for 20–25 minutes.

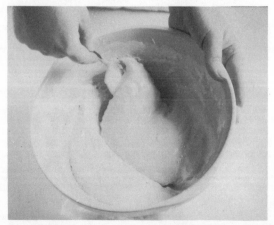

Step 2. Cut in the well sieved flour with a metal spoon. Do this gently so that you just blend in the flour without losing the air already beaten in.

Step 4. Allow the cake a few minutes to shrink from the sides of the tin then carefully turn out onto a wire tray.

POINTS TO BE NOTED:

Eggs should be used at room temperature (*never* use them straight out of the fridge).

Always use caster sugar. Granulated sugar is too coarse and will give the cake a speckled appearance as it does not dissolve when beaten with eggs.

Always use plain flour that is perfectly dry. If you think it may be a little damp, put it in the oven for a little while then sieve at least twice before use.

Make sure the mixing basin and whisk are thoroughly clean and free from grease.

If you use an electric or rotary beater there's no need to beat the mixture over hot water.

SWISS ROLL

Baking time: 7–10 minutes
  2 large (medium) eggs
  2 ounces (50 grams) caster sugar
  2 ounces (50 grams) self-raising flour
  3 level tablespoons warmed jam

Preheat the oven to 425°F, 220°C or Gas Mark 7. Grease and line a 9 by 12-inch Swiss roll tin. Take eggs at room temperature and whisk with sugar until the mixture is light and creamy and the whisk leaves a trail when lifted out of the mixture. Fold in sieved flour using a metal spoon. Turn into prepared tin and smooth level with a palette knife. Bake in a hot oven, 425°F, 220°C or Gas Mark 7, until sponge begins to shrink from the edges of the tin and is pale golden brown, approximately 7–10

minutes. Turn out onto a sheet of greaseproof paper dredged with caster sugar. Trim edges of sponge, spread with jam and roll up tightly. Dredge with caster sugar and cool.

SPONGE FINGERS

Baking time: 12 minutes
  7 ounces (200 grams) plain flour
  pinch of salt
  6 eggs, separated
  7 ounces (200 grams) caster sugar

Preheat the oven to 350°F, 180°C or Gas Mark 4. Prepare a baking sheet by lining with a sheet of greaseproof paper brushed with oil and dust with flour.

Sieve the flour and salt. Cream the egg yolks and sugar together with a wooden spoon or a whisk until light and creamy. Whisk the egg whites until stiff and standing in peaks. Fold about one-third of the carefully sieved flour into the egg yolks then add the egg whites folding carefully with a metal spoon. Finally cut in the remaining flour. Put the mixture into a forcing bag with a plain large nozzle and pipe about $3\frac{1}{2}$-inch long fingers on to the baking sheet. Alternatively you can use sponge finger tins suitably greased and floured. Dust the fingers with icing sugar. Bake for about 12 minutes in a moderate oven, 350°F, 190°C or Gas Mark 4.

Makes 36 sponge fingers.

Swiss Roll

For this scrumptious Strawberry Sponge cover two whisked sponges (see page 48) with sliced, sugared strawberries. Allow these to stand long enough to let the juice soak and then add whipped cream. Place one sponge on top of the other as shown below and serve very cold.

SMALL CAKES

GENOESE PASTRY

Baking time: 30–35 minutes
  3 ounces (75 grams) plain flour
  3 ounces (75 grams) butter, unsalted
  4 (small) eggs
  4 ounces (100 grams) caster sugar

Preheat the oven to 350°F, 180°C or Gas Mark 4. Grease a square 8-inch tin or small Swiss roll tin, then line the bottom with a piece of greaseproof paper, which fits exactly. Dust with caster sugar and then with flour.

Sieve the flour and salt at least twice. Heat the butter gently until it is just soft and will pour; do not make it oily however. Beat the eggs and sugar over hot water as for whisked sponge. If using an electric mixer you do not need the water. Beat the eggs and sugar until they are thick and creamy. This will take about 5–7 minutes depending on whether you use hand or machine. If whisking by hand remove the bowl from the heat and continue whisking for a few minutes until cool. Use a metal spoon to cut in about two-thirds of the sieved flour, then the pouring butter followed by the remaining flour. Turn the mixture into the prepared tin and bake in a moderate oven for 30 minutes.

Use for small cakes or gâteaux.

FRENCH CAKES

  1 slab of Genoese pastry
  1 pound icing sugar
FOR DECORATION:
  crystallised violets
  angelica
  piped butter cream
  chocolate drops, cut
  melted chocolate, piped

Cut the sponge into various shapes. Mark off 1½-inch squares with a ruler or cut rounds with a scone cutter. For the diamonds cut a strip of paper 1½ inches wide then draw two diagonal lines, each measuring 1½ inches, across the width of the paper. Place pattern on a strip of cake 1½ inches wide and you will have uniform diamond shapes. Make up the glacé icing (page 61). Place the small cakes on a wire rack over a plate, plastic tray or clean baking sheet (this ensures that dripped icing may be used again). Follow

Allow the cake to cool and it can be layered as a gâteaux or cut in small diagonal, round, square shapes as directed in the recipe. Brush the small shapes with a clean dry pastry brush to make sure that they are as free from crumbs as possible. Arrange them on the wire tray with a clean, crumb-free tray or plate underneath.

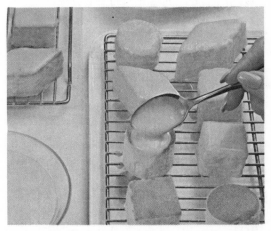

Make up the glacé icing as directed. Cover the cakes with white icing first by pouring a spoonful over each and allow to drip down, a further spoonful will give a better finish. You can then colour the remaining icing with harmless green or pink vegetable colouring. For variety use chocolate coating for some of your small cakes. Crystallised violets with angelica leaves, piped butter cream, yellow mimosa balls, or any of the decorations mentioned in the recipe will finish the cakes for a special occasion.

directions given under the pictures and decorate the tops of the cakes with any of the suggested decorations.

Makes 10–14 cakes depending on the shapes.

Strawberry Cream Sponge

APRICOT BASKETS

Baking time: 15 minutes
  2 ounces (50 grams) margarine
  2 ounces (50 grams) caster sugar
  1 egg
  3 ounces (75 grams) self-raising flour
  1 dessertspoon milk
  1 can apricot halves
  apricot jam
  angelica
  whipped cream, optional

Preheat the oven to 375°F, 190°C or Gas Mark 5. Cream the margarine and sugar together until the mixture is light and fluffy. Add the egg and 1 teaspoon of the flour and beat well. Add the milk and then sieve in the remainder of the flour and salt. Fold in with a metal spoon. Grease 9 small bun tins and divide the mixture equally into each tin. Bake for 15 minutes in a fairly hot oven. Cool on a wire tray. Drain and dry the apricots on a clean towel.

Make a glaze with some apricot jam by sieving and heating. Place the apricots round side up on the buns, and paint with apricot jam glaze. Soften the angelica in warm water cut into strips long enough to arch over the buns as handles. Pipe small rosettes of cream round the baskets.
Makes 9 baskets.

CHOCOLATE ORANGE CREAMS

Baking time: 10 minutes
  1 Swiss roll mixture (page 49)
  apricot or peach jam, heated and sieved
  1 block chocolate meunière
  1 small tin mandarin oranges, drained
  1 small carton double cream,
    whipped stiffly

Allow the sponge to cool unrolled, then spread with apricot jam. Cut in half and sandwich together. Cut into small squares. Melt the chocolate over a bowl of hot water than spread on a piece of waxed paper with a palette knife (thinly). When the chocolate is almost set, mark the squares with a hot knife making the same size as cakes. Spread the four sides with apricot jam and when the chocolate is firmly set dip the knife in boiling water again, cut through the marked lines, lift off the paper then press gently on to the sides of the cakes. Place 2 segments of mandarin oranges on each cake and pipe small rosettes of cream round the oranges.

CHOCOLATE TRUFFLES

Preparation time: 12 minutes
  4 ounces (100 grams) plain chocolate
  4 ounces (100 grams) stale sponge crumbs
  2 ounces (50 grams) ground almonds
  2 ounces (50 grams) caster sugar
  1 tablespoon rum
  1 tablespoon apricot jam
  1 tablespoon chocolate vermicelli

Melt the chocolate in a bowl over some hot water. Put the cake crumbs, ground almonds and the caster sugar in a bowl. Stir in the rum and the chocolate to give a fairly stiff consistency. Form the mixture into 12 balls and roll in chocolate vermicilli. Put in paper cases.
Makes 12 truffles.

COCONUT PYRAMIDS

Baking time: 40 minutes
  3 egg whites
  4 ounces (100 grams) caster sugar
  8 ounces (200 grams) dessicated coconut
  1 tablespoon ground rice

Preheat the oven to 300°F, 150°C or Gas Mark 2. Whisk the egg whites until they are stiff and peaked, then gradually whisk in half of the sugar. Fold in the remaining sugar, coconut and ground rice. Take a dessert spoon of the mixture and shape into a pyramid with a fork. Put on a well-oiled baking sheet or on rice paper if you have any. Bake in a slow oven until pale golden and firm.
Makes 12 pyramids.

BOSTON COFFEE CREAMS

Baking time: 15 minutes
  5 ounces (150 grams) plain flour
  4 ounces (125 grams) butter or margarine
  1 ounce (25 grams) icing sugar
  ¼ teaspoon vanilla essence
  ½ egg

Cream the fat and sugar together. Beat the egg, add half along with the vanilla essence. Mix in sieved flour. Put the mixture into a forcing bag with a large rosette pipe. Pipe onto a greased baking sheet. Bake for 15 minutes. Cool and sandwich together with butter icing flavoured with coffee. Preheat over to 350°F, 180°C or Gas Mark 4.
Makes between two and three dozen cakes.

AMERICAN CAKES

These are different in texture from our own cakes, you will find the mixtures tend to be rather like batter. The frostings are sweet and marshmallow-like but they look marvellous and make tea-time really festive.

PINEAPPLE CHIFFON CAKE

Baking time: 1 hour 5 minutes

**10 ounces (275 grams) extra fine
  plain flour**
3 teaspoons baking powder
1 teaspoon salt
6 tablespoons vegetable oil
5 egg yolks
**6 tablespoons unsweetened
  pineapple juice**
8 egg whites
½ teaspoon cream of tartar

FILLING AND TOPPING:
½ pint (3 decilitres) whipped cream
1 small can crushed pineapple

Preheat the oven to 325°F, 170°C or Gas Mark 3.

Step 1. Sieve the dry ingredients into a bowl about three times then make a well in the centre. Add oil, egg yolks and pineapple juice. Beat until smooth

Step 2. In a large mixing bowl, whisk the egg whites and cream of tartar until they form stiff peaks. Pour the egg yolk batter in a thin stream over the entire surface of the egg whites, gently folding in with a metal spoon until just blended.

Step 3. Bake in an ungreased funnel tin in a slow oven for 55 minutes then turn up the oven to 350°F, 180°C or Gas Mark 4, for an extra 10 minutes. Invert on a bottle, allow to cool, and remove from the tin.

To fill and top add 1 small can of crushed, drained pineapple to the whipped cream.

Chiffon Cake

A cake is more attractive if it is finished with an icing or frosting. I realise that many women have little time to spend on cake decoration; however it is useful to know one or two quick finishes for butter cream. Experiment with a fork to give a "line" finish or a knife will "peak" this type of icing. If time is really pressing then icing sugar sieved over a doiley will give a patterned finish.

Lemon Coconut Cake.

Angel Cake.

ANGEL CAKE

Baking time: 1 hour
  8 egg whites
  7 ounces (200 grams) caster sugar
  ¼ teaspoon vanilla essence
  1 tablespoon water
  4 ounces (125 grams) self-raising flour
  pinch of salt
  ½ teaspoon cream of tartar, extra fine

Preheat the oven to 375°F, 190°C or Gas Mark 5. Use an 8 to 9-inch diameter angel cake tin with a funnel.

Sieve the flour and half of the caster sugar at least three times. In a large, well-polished basin whisk the egg whites, salt and cream of tartar until stiff but not dry. Add the rest of the sugar about a tablespoon at a time then add essence. Continue beating until mixture is very stiff. Fold in carefully with a metal spoon or plastic scraper the flour and sugar. Place the mixture in a clean dry tin and draw a knife through to break the air bubbles. Bake the cake in a preheated oven for 30 minutes until the cake springs back when pressed with a finger. Invert over a bottle to cool then turn onto a wire tray. Dust with icing sugar or use frosting.

LEMON COCONUT CAKE

Baking time: 30–35 minutes
  5 ounces (150 grams) margarine
  6 ounces (175 grams) caster sugar
  2 eggs
  1 teaspoon vanilla
  10 ounces (275 grams) plain flour
  2½ teaspoons baking powder
  1 teaspoon salt
  ½ pint (3 decilitres) milk
FILLING:
  lemon curd

Preheat the oven to 350°F, 177°C or Gas Mark 4. Cream the margarine (use soft luxury margarine) until it becomes soft and light. Add the sugar gradually and cream until light and fluffy. Add the eggs and flavouring with a little of the measured flour if necessary. Sieve the dry ingredients several times (for best results use American cake flour) and add to the creamed mixture alternately with the milk. Beat after each addition and then for about 1 minute. Bake in 2 8–9 inch sandwich tins for 30–35 minutes. Allow to cool for a few minutes then turn on to a wire tray and when completely cool sandwich together with lemon curd.

Finish with Seven Minute frosting on page 57. Frost the sides, then roll in dessicated coconut before frosting the top.
Makes 2 8–9-inch cakes.

FEATHERY FUDGE CAKE

Baking time: 30–35 minutes
  6 ounces (150 grams) soft margarine
  14 ounces (400 grams) caster sugar
  2 eggs
  1 teaspoon vanilla
  2½ ounces (75 grams) bitter chocolate,
    melted
  1¼ teaspoons bicarbonate of soda
  ½ teaspoon salt
  ½ pint ice water

Preheat the oven to 350°F, 180°C or Gas Mark 4. Cream together soft margarine, sugar and eggs for 5 minutes at high speed in the mixer. Scrape down the bowl from time to time. Blend in the cooled melted chocolate. Sieve together the flour, soda and salt; add alternately with the ice water beating after each addition. Bake in 2 greased and lined tins for 30 to 35 minutes. Frost with Chocolate Fudge Icing and sprinkle with chopped walnuts.
Makes 2 8-inch cakes.

DEVIL'S FOOD CAKE

Baking time: 30 minutes
  4 ounces (100 grams) shortening
  9 ounces (225 grams) caster sugar
  5 ounces (125 grams) extra fine
    plain flour
  ½ teaspoon baking powder
  1 teaspoon bicarbonate of soda
  pinch of salt
  2 ounces (50 grams) cocoa
  2 eggs
  12 tablespoons water

Preheat the oven to 350°F, 180°C or Gas Mark 4. Grease and flour two 7-inch sandwich tins.

Cream the shortening and sugar until light and fluffy. Whisk the eggs lightly and gradually beat into shortening and sugar. Sieve the dry ingredients and cut in with a metal spoon. Cook in the preheated oven for 30 minutes. Decorate with Chocolate fudge icing (see page 61).

AMERICAN PEACH CRUMB CAKE

Baking time: 45 minutes
  BASE:
  2 ounces (50 grams) butter
  3 ounces (75 grams) soft brown sugar
  2 eggs
  5 ounces (125 grams) self raising flour
  3 (2) tablespoons milk

TOPPING:
  1 can peaches, sliced and drained
  4 ounces (100 grams) butter
  4 ounces (100 grams) caster sugar
  4 ounces (100 grams) plain flour

Preheat the oven, 350°F, 175°C or Gas Mark 4. To make the base, cream together the butter and sugar until soft and fluffy. Beat in the eggs one at a time. Stir in the four and milk to form a stiff batter. Pour the batter into a greased and lined 7-inch shallow cake tin. Place the peaches over the batter.

To make the topping, rub the butter into the flour and sugar until the mixture resembles breadcrumbs. Sprinkle the mixture over the peaches. Bake in a preheated oven for 45 minutes, 40 minutes for metric recipe. Allow to cool in the tin and cut into slices to serve. Delicious served with whipped cream as a dessert.

ICINGS AND FROSTINGS

SEVEN MINUTE FROSTING

Cooking time: 7 minutes
  2 egg whites
  7 ounces (200 grams) icing sugar
  ¼ teaspoon cream of tartar
  4 tablespoons water
  pinch of salt
  1 teaspoon vanilla essence

Put all the ingredients in the top of a double boiler (not over the heat yet). Beat for 1 minute with the rotary or electric mixer.

Now put the mixture on top of boiling water and beat constantly till frosting forms stiff peaks (should be about 7 minutes). Remove from the heat, add the vanilla and beat to a spreading consistency (about another 2 minutes).
  Makes frosting for the top and sides of two 8 to 9-inch cakes sandwiched together.

Fill the inside of the cake first before beginning the frosting then put a thin coat over the sides to make sure there are no stray crumbs. Lastly, decorate the top.

COFFEE FROSTING

  1 pound (450 grams) granulated sugar
  12 tablespoons water
  **1 teaspoon instant coffee, made up in
    2 teaspoons water**
  2 egg whites

Put the sugar and water in a thick saucepan and allow to dissolve over a low heat. Brush down any crystals which appear above the level of the liquid. *Do not stir.* When the sugar has dissolved, add the coffee liquid and allow to boil fast, again without stirring. Boil to 240°F, 115°C, if you have a sugar thermometer or until the sugar just begins to spin a 6-inch thread. Whisk the egg white until stiff and peaky. Pour on the hot syrup in a thin stream, holding the pan at a good height and whisking briskly all the time. When the icing begins to look like shiny cotton wool, spread quickly on the cake with sweeping strokes. Decorate the sides of the cake with halved walnuts.

RICH CHOCOLATE ICING

  3 egg whites
  12 ounces (325 grams) icing sugar
  4 ounces (100 grams) softened butter
  2 ounces (50 grams) cocoa
  ½ teaspoon vanilla
  **2 ounces (50 grams) halved almonds,
    toasted**

For this icing a small mixer or rotary whisk gives quicker results—otherwise it is a *labour* of love!
  In a larger bowl beat the butter until very creamy and soft. Mix the cocoa with the icing sugar and gradually beat into the butter. Flavour with the essence but if it is for a special cake try a little rum or orange curacao. Beat the egg whites until they stand in peaks. Gradually beat in half of the icing sugar until mixture is stiffly peaked. Fold in the meringue mixture to the butter and blend well.
  Fill and ice the outside of the cake with this icing.
Makes enough to fill and cover an 8-inch cake.

7 Minute Frosting for this tempting cake.

BUTTER ICING

>   4 ounces (100 grams) butter
>   8 ounces (200 grams) icing sugar
>   flavouring

Cream the butter with a wooden spoon, until white and fluffy. Sieve the sugar and add to the butter gradually beating with a wooden spoon. If it is too stiff it may remove the surface of your cake therefore add a little milk if you need a softer icing.

FLAVOURINGS TO ADD TO BUTTER ICING
>   2 tablespoons cocoa blended with
>   2 tablespoons boiling water
>   for chocolate
>   1 tablespoon instant coffee blended
>   with 2 tablespoons boiling water
>   for coffee
>   chocolate and coffee flavour together
>   make Mocha icing
>   2 tablespoons orange or lemon juice
>   and a little rind
>   colourings may be added with
>   flavourings

CONFECTIONER'S CUSTARD

>   2 egg yolks
>   1 egg white
>   2 ounces (50 grams) caster sugar
>   1 level teaspoon plain flour
> $\frac{1}{2}$ pint (3 decilitres) milk
>   1 vanilla pod

Whip the two egg yolks and sugar together until creamy. Blend the flour and cornflour with a little cold milk until a smooth paste is obtained. Infuse the remaining milk with a vanilla pod. Add the flour paste to the egg yolk mixture and blend until smooth. Remove the vanilla pod and save it for the next time. Pour the milk over the egg mixture then return all of the mixture to the pan. Stir over gentle heat until the mixture boils and thickens. I find a hand whisk ensures that no lumps form as the mixture thickens. Whip the egg white until stiff and peaky then add a little of the thickened boiling cream to the egg white then fold this into the cream. Turn into a bowl to cool and keep until needed.

Use for filling choux pastry or pastry cases as an added variety in place of whipped cream.
Makes $\frac{1}{2}$ pint confectioner's custard.

GLACE ICING (simple)

8 ounces (225 grams) icing sugar
4 tablespoons warm water

Sieve icing sugar into a bowl, gradually stir in the water and beat well. Flavouring or colouring can be added to the icing as desired.

Chocolate Glacé Icing

add 2 ounces (50 grams) melted chocolate to the above quantity

For a very glossy glacé icing use:

8 ounces (200 grams) icing sugar
4 tablespoons syrup made from sugar and water

Boil 2 tablespoons sugar and $\frac{1}{4}$ pint water in a small saucepan for about 10 minutes. Remove the pan from the heat and when quite cold add the icing sugar a little at a time, beat thoroughly with a wooden spatula. The icing should coat the back of the spoon and look glossy. Warm the pan slightly on a very low heat then flavour the icing and spread with a palette knife.
Note: Do not use a wet palette knife to spread the icing or it will lose its gloss. Dip the knife in boiling water but dry on a paper towel after each dip.

FONDANT ICING

1 pound (450 grams) icing sugar
1 large egg white
2 tablespoons of liquid glucose

Sieve the icing sugar into a large basin. Add the egg white and glucose (this is obtainable from most chemists). Beat the icing until all the icing sugar is completely mixed with the liquid and makes a large "doughlike" lump. Turn out onto a board sprinkled with icing sugar and knead until smooth and pliable. If colouring is required knead in a few drops at the beginning of the kneading process. Apply in the same way as Almond Paste is put on a cake, by rolling and cutting to fit the shape of the cake.

Take a 12 inch square of greaseproof paper

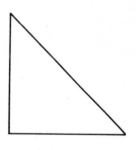

Fold paper into a triangle

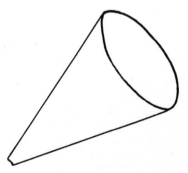

Fold into a coronet. Cut off a small tip.

Royal Icing on Christmas Cake.

ALMOND PASTE

8 ounces (200 grams) ground almonds
10 ounces (250 grams) icing sugar
1 egg white
2 teaspoons orange flower water
a few drops of lemon juice

Mix the sugar and ground almonds together. Make a well in the centre and add the egg whites and flavourings (I sometimes use 2 egg yolks to mix but it is a matter of individual taste). Mix with small palette-knife and take to a smooth paste.

ROYAL ICING

3 egg whites
juice of 1 lemon strained
1½ pounds (675 grams) icing sugar
1 teaspoon of glycerine

Beat the egg whites for about ½ minute with an electric mixer or a rotary or hand whisk. Continue beating, adding the icing sugar until the mixture stands in soft peaks. Add the glycerine to prevent the royal icing from becoming rock hard.

For piping add a little more icing sugar until the mixture stands in sharp peaks.

TO DECORATE A CAKE

A rich fruit cake which is to be used for a birthday, wedding or Christmas cake must be covered with a layer of almond paste to protect the icing from cake crumbs.

To cover a cake with almond paste first brush the sides with sieved apricot jam. Roll out the almond paste on a board dusted with icing sugar to a long narrow strip, the width of the sides of the cake. Trim the edges straight and make sure that your strip fits the circumference of the cake. Roll around the sides like a bandage. To begin with you may find it easier to handle half the strip at a time. Join the edges and run round the sides with an upright rolling pin.

Roll out remaining paste to a circle the size of the top of the cake. I use the bottom of the cake tin as a guide for size otherwise draw a circle on a piece of paper to fit the top of the cake. Brush the top of the cake with sieved apricot jam and place the round on top. Use a rolling pin or palette knife to smooth the join between top and sides. After making sure the cake is as smooth as possible, leave to dry for about 2 days before icing. To apply the Royal Icing put the cake on a board then place on top of an upturned cake tin. Put half the icing on top of the cake and work to and fro with a palette knife. Smooth the top with the edge of palette knife or metal ruler held with two hands and drawn across the cake towards you. If a smooth icing is required on the sides allow the top to dry first. Ice the sides by spreading with the icing and drawing a vertical knife or ruler round the cake. Allow to dry and decorate or pipe as desired. For a 'peaked' finish spread icing all over and peak with small round topped knife. Coloured ribbons tied round the sides make an attractive and easy finish.

Fork Finish

For a quick easy finish to a cake iced with butter cream icing use a fork which has been dipped in boiling water and then dried on a tissue. Obtain a "feather" effect by using the fork across the cake as shown in the picture. Alternatively pull the fork round the cake in ever-decreasing circles then divide into portions by drawing the fork across the cake in a cross. Decorate with Smarties, chocolate drops, crystallised violets.

To Make Brazil Nut Daisies

Cover unshelled Brazil nuts with cold water, simmer for 3 minutes then allow to drain. Stand in cold water for about 1 minute, drain and shell. Cover nuts with cold water, simmer for 3 minutes and drain. Cut paper thin, lengthwise slices with a vegetable parer. Use as petals round glacé cherries to make daisies.

UNCOOKED CHOCOLATE FUDGE FROSTING

2 ounces (50 grams) chocolate
8 ounces (225 grams) icing sugar
3 tablespoons milk
1 egg
1 teaspoon vanilla essence
2 ounces (50 grams) softened butter

Melt the chocolate in a bowl over hot water and then allow to cool slightly. Take a milk saucepan tip in the sieved icing sugar then add the milk, egg and vanilla. A better flavour is obtained if you can infuse the milk with a vanilla pod.

Step 1. Stir in the chocolate and add the softened butter (not melted) a little at a time. Chill in the refrigerator for 10 minutes.

Step 2. Place pan over a bowl of water with ice. Holding the handle of the pan, beat the frosting until it is the correct spreading consistency. Makes enough frosting for 1 8-inch square cake.

MERINGUES

5

Meringues are a mixture of egg white and sugar and are very easy to make. They're a great favourite with anyone who has a sweet tooth. There are several types of meringues.

Meringue suisse—this is the most common one which is used for meringue shells which are filled with whipped cream.

Meringue cuite—this is a firmer type of meringue which is used for meringue baskets. Icing sugar is used in place of caster.

Meringue italienne—this is rather specialised. Loaf sugar is made into a syrup and the use of a sugar thermometer is necessary before it is poured on to the beaten egg whites.

I shall only mention the first two of these as they cover most household needs.

Meringue shell filled with strawberry ice cream and strawberries.

MERINGUE SHELLS

Baking time: 1½ hours

3 egg whites
6 ounces (175 grams) caster sugar
FILLING:
whipped cream

Preheat the oven to 250°F, 120°C or Gas Mark 1. Brush two baking sheets with oil, dredge with flour and then shake off the excess. Whisk the egg whites until they stand up in peaks. Whisk in one tablespoon of the sugar for about 1 minute. Fold in the remaining sugar as quickly as possible with a metal spoon. Spoon out the meringue onto a tray or use a piping bag with a plain nozzle and pipe the meringue in rounds. Dust with caster sugar then place in the oven. If you have two trays on separate shelves, change them round after half an hour. When the meringues are set, take them carefully off the sheet with a sharp knife and slightly press in the underside. Replace them on the baking sheet, laying them on their sides, and let them dry out for about 20 minutes in the oven. Finally, take out of the oven and allow to cool on a wire rack. Once the meringue has been filled with cream it must be eaten within a few hours.
Makes 6 filled meringues.

This kind of meringue is also used as a pudding topping.

Lemon Meringue Pie

Baking time: 1 hour

1 8-inch short-pastry flan (pages 67–68)
FILLING:
3 lemons
8 ounces (250 grams) caster sugar
1½ ounces (45 grams) cornflour
3 eggs separated
½ pint (3 decilitres) water

Preheat the oven to 325°F, 160°C or Gas Mark 3. Make pastry flan as directed on pages 67–68. To make filling put egg yolks in a bowl with 3 ounces of the caster sugar over hot water and whisk. Grate the rinds of 2 lemons, squeeze the juice of all 3, add and allow to cook. Gently blend cornflour with a little cold water. Whick in the egg yolks and sugar mixture. Allow to thicken. Whisk the egg whites until they are like cotton wool. Whisk in 1 tablespoon of sugar and whisk until mixture is stiff

and shining. Add the remaining sugar and fold in with a metal spoon. Fill a cold pastry case with cold sauce or warm case with warm sauce. Pile on the meringue and put back in the middle of a moderately hot oven until the meringue begins to crisp on top.
Makes 6 portions.

1. Use a rotary whisk or electric mixer to whisk egg whites. Make sure that all bowls and utensils are absolutely free from grease.

2. Whisk the egg whites to a stiff firm snow. Quickly whisk in 1 tablespoon of sugar and continue whisking until meringue is glossy. Remove the whisk and fold in remaining sugar with a spatula.

3. Seal the meringue to the filling and pastry case with a knife. Swirl the meringue by spreading with the knife. Pipe meringue on top if preferred. Bake according to recipe directions.

Baked Alaska Pudding

1 sponge cake
2 tablespoons sherry (optional)
1 family brick ice-cream
4 egg whites
8 ounces (250 grams) icing sugar

Follow step by step pictures in the right-hand column. Sprinkle sherry on sponge cake before placing the ice-cream in position.

STUFFED PEACH MERINGUES

This is a delicious sweet for a dinner party when peaches are in season.

Baking time: 45 minutes

1 large peach per person

FILLING FOR EACH PEACH:
1 teaspoon fresh white breadcrumbs
1 teaspoon ground almonds
1 teaspoon icing sugar
stiffly beaten egg white to mix

SYRUP FOR POACHING THE PEACHES:
½ pint (3 decilitres) water
6 ounces (160 grams) granulated sugar

MERINGUE:
(allow 2 egg whites to top every
3 peaches)
1 egg white
generous 2 ounces (60 grams)
icing sugar

Preheat the oven to 325°F, 160°C or Gas Mark 3. Peel the peaches. Cut a small piece from the bottom of the peaches so that they will stand in an ovenproof dish. Scoop out the stone without splitting the fruit. Mix the filling together and blend with some stiffly beaten egg white and stuff the hole left by the stone. Pour the syrup round the fruit, add a few drops of brandy if possible. Poach in a moderate oven for 15 minutes. For the meringue, sieve the icing sugar and tip it into the stiffly beaten egg whites and whisk over hot water (no hot water needed if an electric whisk is used) until the mixture is stiff and peaky. Pipe or mound on top of the peaches so that each has a smart little hat of meringue. Return the peaches to the oven without slopping the syrup. Allow meringues to crisp in the oven for about 30 minutes. Remove carefully onto the serving dish.

1. Trim a layer of sponge cake or layer cake on cutting board 1 inch bigger on all sides than the block of ice cream. Add fruit if desired. Make meringue.

2. Gradually add caster sugar to the stiffly beaten egg whites; beat till peaks form. Now place 1 block brick ice cream on the cake.

3. Spread meringue over ice cream cake, sealing well to the cake. Bake at 450°F, 230°C or Gas Mark 8 about 5 minutes. Slide on to a plate—paper strips underneath help. Better still arrange the whole pudding on an ovenproof dish.

MERINGUE BASKETS

Baking time: 45 minutes
4 egg whites
pinch of salt
generous 8 ounces (240 grams)
icing sugar

Preheat the oven to 300°F, 150°C or Gas Mark 2. Beat the egg whites in a basin until foamy then add the sieved icing sugar a little at a time until it is all added to the egg whites. If using an electric mixer continue to beat until the mixture forms a stiff ribbon when dropped from a spoon. However if a hand whisk is being used place the bowl over a saucepan of hot water add the icing sugar and beat until thick. Place a tablespoon of the mixture on to a piece of greaseproof paper which has circles drawn round a 2-inch cutter or with a compass and then oil the paper. Work the mixture into the centre with a spoon until a hollow is formed in the middle. This method is for my friends who swear the sight of a piping bag reduces them to a state of "fingers and thumbs". Truly it is much easier to toss the mixture into a piping bag with a large star or plain pipe and shape the circle and then carefully build up 2 rings to form a wall. When piping the larger baskets it is better to pipe the wall and the bottom separately and join together after cooking. Bake the baskets in the preheated oven for 40–50 minutes. Meringue should be crisped on the outside and rather gooey inside. If you want the meringue to remain white then use a slower temperature for a longer time.

Fill the baskets with a mixture of strawberries, raspberries or other fruit and cream. Mandarin oranges dipped in caramel sugar (page 84) is a delicious sweet filling. Both small and large baskets can be filled with ice cream and fruit.

FAULTS IN MERINGUE MAKING:
Meringues are such a favourite with the sweet-toothed that even the ones which are not quite as handsome as they might be are quickly eaten.
Meringues which are sticky can be caused by:
1. Insufficient beating of the egg whites
2. Too much caster sugar added at once.
Tough meringues can be caused by:
1. Too much sugar and the folding of the sugar has not fully incorporated it into the egg whites.

STRAWBERRY MERINGUE CAKE

Baking time: 1 hour 5 minutes for the two stages
1 basic whisked sponge
MERINGUE RINGS:
4 egg whites
pinch of salt
8 ounces (225 grams) caster sugar
FILLING:
½ pint (3 decilitres) thick cream,
whipped
1 pound (500 grams) strawberries

Preheat the oven to 275°F, 140°C or Gas Mark 1. Make the sponge as on page 48. Allow to cool on a wire tray.
Beat the egg whites and salt until stiff and peaky. Add half the caster sugar and beat until the mixture is stiff; this will take about a minute. Fold in the remaining caster sugar with a metal spoon. Now cut two pieces of non-stick paper to the size of the cake. Put the meringue into a forcing bag with a plain vegetable pipe. Pipe on to one sheet so that it is completely covered. Pipe a wall round the edge of the other sheet so that a hole is left in the middle for the strawberries. Bake in a slow oven for about 1 hour. Lift the rings from the paper.

Hull the strawberries and sprinkle with caster sugar. Halve the sponge cake. Spread some cream on the bottom half of the cake. Place the sheet of meringue on top of the cream then add strawberries and cream round the edge as shown. Place the other half of the cake on top. Spread thinly with cream then place the meringue ring in place. Fill the centre of the ring with fruit and cream.

With a compass draw a circle 2½" in diameter on a piece of paper. Brush paper with oil then sprinkle with caster sugar. Position 2 spoonfuls of meringue and work into a shell with a spoon as shown below.

PASTRY

6

Really good pastry is delicious and is not difficult to produce if you follow a few simple rules.

1. Make pastry at the beginning of your baking when you and the kitchen are cool.
2. Run wrists under the cold tap before rubbing in.
3. Lift the mixture up and crumble the fat into the flour to incorporate air.

4. Sieve the PLAIN flour well and add correct amount of ice-cold water to make a good consistency. Too much water will make hard pastry.
5. Use a wooden rolling pin without handles.
6. Leave pastry aside for twenty minutes before use to avoid shrinkage when cooked.

SHORTCRUST PASTRY

Baking time as stated in individual recipes.
    8 ounces (225 grams) plain flour
    pinch of salt
    4–5 ounces (100–125 grams) butter,
      white fat, lard or margarine
    (I usually use a mixture of both)
    4 tablespoons cold water

Sieve the flour (self-raising flour gives a spongy pastry which some people prefer) with the salt into the mixing bowl. Cut the fat into the flour in small pieces, mix round with a palette knife and then rub in with the tips of the fingers, until the mixture looks like fine breadcrumbs (see pictures of scone making, page 24 for this step).

    Make a well in the centre of the mixture and add the water gradually to make sure you have a firm dough which should leave the sides of bowl completely clean (too much water results in hard pastry). Turn on to a floured board and knead lightly until smooth then allow to stand in a cool place for at least 20 minutes until required.

RICH SHORTCRUST PASTRY

    8 ounces (225 grams) plain flour
    pinch of salt
    5–6 ounces (150 grams) butter
    1 dessertspoon caster sugar
    1 egg yolk
    2–3 tablespoons cold water

Sieve the flour with the salt and rub in the butter as in the method for Shortcrust Pastry, (page 72). After the butter is "rubbed in", add the caster sugar. Make a well in the centre of the flour, mix the egg yolk with the water and tip into the well.

Mix lightly and firmly with a palette knife to a firm dough. Knead lightly on a floured board and allow to stand in a cool place wrapped in grease-proof paper for at least 20 minutes before use.

CHEESE PASTRY

Baking time: 20–25 minutes
    8 ounces (225 grams) plain flour
    4 ounces (100 grams) butter or margarine
    1 ounce (25 grams) grated cheese
    ½ teaspoon salt
    1 egg yolk
    2 tablespoons water

Rub fat into flour and salt following instructions as for Shortcrust Pastry, (page 72). Add the cheese. Make a well in the centre, mix with egg and water, and add a little at a time until a firm dough is obtained. Allow the pastry to rest for a while in the refrigerator. Roll out and line a flan ring or pie plate. Prick the bottom with a fork.
Makes 1 9-inch flan or 2 6-inch flans.

Blackberry Flan decorated with pastry shapes and crumb topping.

To Flute the Edge of a Fruit Pie.
Press the dough with the back of a small round handled knife against a wedge made with the finger and thumb of one hand.

To Make this Petalled Finish on a Pie.
To make this finish on a fruit pie trim the edges $\frac{1}{2}$ inch beyond the edge of the pie. Pinch the bottom and top edges together then cut scallops round the edge with a teaspoon. Brush top with a little milk.

To Divide a Sweet or Savoury Pie into Portions.
Seal the edge with the back of a fork and divide pastry into portions using a pastry wheel.

To Make a Flan

A flan is an open pastry case which can be cooked, stored in an airtight tin, and used when needed filled with sweet or savoury fillings. A flan is better made in a flan ring which is easily available from hardware shops. However it can be made in a sandwich tin but, if using a sandwich tin, allow pastry to cool before removing to avoid breakages.

TO LINE A FLAN RING·

1. Put the flan ring on a flat baking sheet without edges.

2. Roll out the "rested" pastry (see instructions for allowing pastry to stand before use, page 66) to $\frac{1}{4}$–$\frac{1}{2}$-inch thick. Using a knife gently "knock" the sides of the pastry and turn it to obtain a round shape. Roll with light forward strokes and keep rolling until pastry is $1\frac{1}{2}$ inches larger all round the flan ring.

3. Lift the pastry on the rolling pin, lay over the flan ring and ease down into the ring. *Do not stretch the pastry* at this stage or it will shrink when cooked.

4. Bend the top of the pastry over the top of the flan ring and roll off the excess pastry with a rolling pin.

5. Mark round the edges with a fork or pinch with the forefinger and thumb.

Make Your Own Flan

If you don't find exactly the right fruit combination you are looking for amongst recipes in a cookery book try experimenting with fillings for yourself. Thicken 4 cups of fresh fruit or 3 cups of cooked fruit to fill a 9-inch flan. Let the thickened fruit stand for 15 minutes before filling the flan and baking, or alternatively add fruit to already baked pie crust. Correct the sweetening to taste.

Some suggestions are:

$\frac{1}{3}$ **gooseberry and** $\frac{2}{3}$ **strawberry**
$\frac{1}{2}$ **cherry and** $\frac{1}{2}$ **rhubarb**
$\frac{1}{3}$ **cranberry and** $\frac{2}{3}$ **apple**
$\frac{1}{2}$ **apple and** $\frac{1}{2}$ **pear**
$\frac{1}{2}$ **fresh strawberries and** $\frac{1}{2}$ **bananas,**
    with sugar and whipped cream

To Make a Lattice Pie.
Place 7 ½-inch pastry strips across the filling. Weave first cross strip through centre. Fold back alternate strips each time you add a cross strip.

TO BAKE A FLAN "BLIND"

It is possible to cook some mixtures and fruit in a raw pastry flan e.g. apples, plums, or stoned fruits, savoury mixtures such as bacon and egg, fish and sauce mixtures. However most fruits are better arranged in a flan case when it has been cooked.

1. If you have time allow the pastry filled flan ring to stand for 20–30 minutes in the refrigerator.
2. Line pastry with greaseproof paper and half fill the flan with dried beans which can be used again and again.
3. Cook in a preheated oven 400°F, 200°C or Gas Mark 6.
4. Cook the flan on the second top shelf for about 20 minutes then remove from the oven and take out the paper and beans. Carefully remove the flan ring and return to the oven until golden. Cool on a wire rack.

Flans can be filled with any type of fresh or poached fruit. If filled when cold they are normally glazed to give an attractive finish.

Arrowroot glaze made with 1 heaped teaspoon arrowroot to ½ pint fruit juice. Blend the arrowroot with some of the cold juice, boil the remainder add to the cold mixture, return to the pan and allow to thicken. Pour over the fruit.

Apricot jam glaze is made by heating the jam in a saucepan. Add 2–3 tablespoons water and a little lemon juice. Bring to the boil slowly, strain, return to the pan and simmer until thick, brush over flan. Make enough to keep in a jar for the next few times.

For a *red glaze*, heat red currant jelly and brush over the fruit.

For a Twisted Lattice Finish on a Fruit or Syrup Tart.
Twist ¼-inch strips as they are placed on the filling, then place cross strips diagonally twisting as you weave.

DEEP DISH APPLE PIE

Baking time: 35–40 minutes
- **8 ounces (225 grams) rich shortcrust pastry**
- **2 pounds (1 kilo.) cooking apples, peeled, cored and sliced thinly**
- **4 ounces (125 grams) sugar**
- **1 tablespoon honey**
- **4 tablespoons boiling water**
- **4 slices processed cheese (optional)**

Preheat the oven to 400°F, 200°C or Gas Mark 6. Place the peeled, cored and sliced fruit in a deep pie dish, add sugar, honey and water, cover with cheese. Roll out pastry at least 1½ inches larger than pie dish. Cut off extra piece and place this on dampened rim of pie dish. Moisten this border of pastry and place over it the pastry lid. Press gently round edge to seal, and trim off excess pastry. Mark edge firmly with finger and back of knife. Use oddments of pastry for decoration and glaze pastry with egg and milk mixture. Cook in centre of the oven for 35–40 minutes, or until fruit is tender.

APRICOT TARTS

Baking time: 15 minutes
- **8 ounces (225 grams) rich shortcrust pastry**
CREAM FILLING:
- **1 tablespoon plain flour**
- **2 ounces (50 grams) caster sugar**
- **2 egg yolks**
- **¼ pint (1½ decilitres) milk**
- **¼ pint (1½ decilitres) apricot juice**
- **1 can apricot halves**

GLAZE:

4 tablespoons apricot jam
1 tablespoon water

Preheat the oven to 375°F, 190°C or Gas Mark 5. Make up the pastry and line the bottom of 12 patty tins. Prick the bottoms well. Mix sugar and flour, add egg yolk and 1 tablespoon of milk to make a smooth paste. Bring the milk and juice to the boil and pour over the blended mixture, whisking well. Return to the saucepan and cook gently until thick, stirring all the time. Cool.

Divide the filling equally between the pastry cases. Place drained apricot halves on top and bake in a fairly hot oven for about 15 minutes on the second shelf. For the glaze, bring jam and water to the boil for a few minutes, stirring all the time. Sieve and brush over the hot tarts.

Makes 12 tarts.

GRAPE BOATS

First make the 6 ounces (175 grams) shortcrust pastry into boat shaped cases using barquette tins. Bake blind for 10–15 minutes in a moderate oven 350°F, 180°C or Gas Mark 4. Allow to cool and fill with a little Confectioner's Custard (page 58) or a little whipped cream. Arrange grapes on top and glaze with apricot glaze (see above). Alternatively, use Frosted Grapes (page 71). Sails can be made with white paper and masts are made with cocktail sticks. Makes 10 boats.

FRENCH APPLE TART

Baking time: 30 minutes

8 ounces (225 grams) rich shortcrust
pastry
2 pounds (1 kilo.) firm *eating* apples,
peeled and cored
sieved apricot jam
2 tablespoons sugar
8 tablespoons water

Preheat the oven to 375°F, 190°C or Gas Mark 5. Roll out the pastry in an oblong and line the inside of a buttered swiss roll tin. Peel and core the apples saving some of the peelings, drop them into a bowl of cold water as you peel. Slice the apples into thin half moons and lay them in overlapping rows. Place the next row facing in the opposite direction, repeating until the tin is full. Now put the tart straight into the oven so that the moisture from the apples does not go through the pastry. Meanwhile cook the sugar, apple peelings and apricot jam together in a saucepan until it is reduced and a yellowish syrup is produced when the mixture is sieved. Pour the hot syrup on to the apples to glaze. If the thought of boiling syrup and apple peelings seems too much then brush the tart over with hot sieved apricot jam.

Makes 6–8 portions.

Grape Boats make an attractive party table.

Peach, Strawberry and Blackcurrant Tarts.

TARTE À L'ALSACIENNE

Baking time: 50 minutes
I was given this recipe by a marvellous Belgian cook who has a restaurant in Spa.

1 French apple tart (see previous recipe)
¼ pint (1½ decilitres) thick cream
2 egg yolks
1 tablespoon sugar
1 tablespoon Kirsch (optional)

Preheat the oven to 400°F, 210°C or Gas Mark 6. Cook the tart for 15 minutes and while it is cooking, whisk up the cream, eggs and sugar. Add Kirsch if you are lucky enough to have any. Now remove the tart out of the oven and pour the cream mixture over the apples and finish baking in a moderate oven, 350°F, 180°C or Gas Mark 4, until the cream mixture is set and golden brown.

MINCE PIES

Baking time: 20–25 minutes
8 ounces (225 grams) rich shortcrust
pastry or rough puff pastry (page 67)
10 ounces (275 grams) mincemeat

Preheat the oven to 400°F, 200°C or Gas Mark 6 (450°F, 210°C or Gas Mark 8 for rough puff). Use ungreased patty tins to make the mince pies. Roll out the pastry thinly and cut into 24 rounds a little larger than the patty or bun tins. Line the tins with half the rounds of pastry. Place a heaped teaspoon of mincemeat in each tin. Brush round the edge of the remaining pastry with water then place the dampened rounds on top of the mince-meat and seal gently. Flake the edges with the back of a knife if necessary. Make 2–3 slits across each pie. Brush over with milk. Bake on second top shelf about 20 minutes until golden brown. Sprinkle with caster or icing sugar while hot.
Makes 10–12 pies.

To Frost Grapes.
Combine slightly beaten egg white and a little water; brush over clusters of grapes then sprinkle with granulated sugar. Allow to dry on a rack.

MINCEMEAT

Maturing time: at least 2 weeks
  8 ounces (225 grams) currants
  4 ounces (100 grams) raisins, stoned
  4 ounces (100 grams) sultanas
  4 ounces (100 grams) mixed peel
  8 ounces (200 grams) apples, peeled,
    cored and chopped finely
  the rind and juice of 1 lemon
  4 ounces (100 grams) margarine or butter
  4 ounces (100 grams) sugar
  $\frac{1}{4}$ teaspoon mixed spice
  $\frac{1}{2}$ teaspoon ground ginger
  $\frac{1}{2}$ teaspoon cinnamon
  pinch of salt
  4 tablespoons brandy or use extra
    lemon juice

Make sure fruit is clean and dry, then mix well in a bowl. Melt the butter in a saucepan and add all other ingredients to the fruit in the bowl. Mix well then add the melted butter. Cover over the top of the fruit with tin foil or double greaseproof and leave overnight for fruit to swell slightly. Next day, stir well and put the mixture into jars leaving a little space at the top for further swelling. Cover with jam pot covers. Allow the mincemeat to mature for at least 2 weeks before using.
Makes 2 pounds.

CORNISH PASTIES

Baking time: 1 hour
SHORTCRUST PASTRY:
  4 ounces (100 grams) plain flour
  pinch salt
  2 ounces (50 grams) butter or margarine
  2 ounces (50 grams) lard or cooking fat
  2 teaspoons egg yolk
  2 teaspoons cold water
FILLING:
  4 ounces (100 grams) top rump
    (or other lean steak)
  1 good-sized potato
  1 small onion
  salt and pepper

Preheat the oven to 400°F, 200°C or Gas Mark 6. Make the pastry by rubbing the fat into the salted flour with your fingertips, until the mixture resembles fine breadcrumbs. Add the egg and

Mince Pies.

water; mix to a firm dough which leaves the sides of the bowl clean. Roll to an 8-inch round.

Cut the meat into small thin pieces, chop the onion finely, cut the potato into thin slices and then into sticks. Spread two-thirds of the potato sticks onto the pastry, then the meat and then the rest on the potato, seasoning each layer as you go along (1 teaspoon of Worcester sauce and 1 teaspoon chopped parsley or chervil add to the flavour).

Damp the edges of the pastry with cold water and fold over to form a semicircle. Crimp the edge of the pastry with your fingers. Now stand the pasty on a baking sheet so that the join goes over the top. Make a small slit for the steam to escape. Brush over with egg and bake in a hot oven for 20 minutes on the second top shelf. Reduce the heat to 350°F, 170°C or Gas Mark 4, place in the middle of the oven and cook for a further 40 minutes.
Makes 1 large or 2 small pasties.

Cornish Pasties.

BACON AND EGG FLAN

This is a popular stand-by if you have casual callers who stay until they need feeding. I always keep some short pastry ready "rubbed in" in a polythene bag in the 'fridge. All you have to do is tip it into a bowl add water or egg yolk and water and roll out. It is much quicker and less messy than making sandwiches.

Baking time: 30–40 minutes

8 ounces (225 grams) shortcrust pastry
4–6 rashers of bacon
4–5 eggs
salt and pepper
2 ounces (50 grams) sliced mushrooms (optional)
1 large skinned sliced tomato (optional)
freshly chopped parsley (optional)

Preheat the oven to 400°F, 200°C or Gas Mark 6. Remove the rind from the bacon, dice and fry lightly (do not overcook). Take a flan ring or a sandwich tin and line as instructed on page 69, but do not trim. Use two-thirds of the pastry, saving the last third for a lid. Arrange some of the chopped bacon on the bottom of the flan, break the eggs carefully into a cup then slip them into the pastry case, *whole*. Mushrooms and tomatoes can be divided, some below some above the eggs. Sprinkle the remaining bacon on top, then sprinkle with salt, pepper and parsley. Roll out the lid slightly larger than the ring. Brush the edge of the flan pastry with water and lift lid on rolling pin placing carefully on top. Seal the edges gently by trimming round with the rolling pin. Make a hole in the centre or slits to allow steam to escape but try not to break the eggs. Brush over with beaten egg and bake on the second top shelf for 30–40 minutes.

Makes 6 portions.

BISCUIT CRUST PASTRY

Mixed and pressed into a tin, these crusts are a shortcut to making pies. They need not be baked before filling, but If used unbaked must first be chilled thoroughly, otherwise the filling will cause the crust to disintegrate. If baked before filling they require 15 minutes in a 300°F oven. It is best to cool the empty baked pie shell before filling.

As an extra-special treat add almonds and cream to the cinnamon and melted butter already in the crushed biscuits.

8 ounces (200 grams) digestive biscuits, crushed
4 ounces (100 grams) butter
pinch ground cinnamon

Melt the butter in a small saucepan. Add the biscuit crumbs and cinnamon and mix well. Press the mixture over the base and sides of an 8-inch pie dish. Chill in the refrigerator until firm.

LEMON FILLING
¼ pint (1½ decilitres) lemon juice
½ ounce (15 grams) gelatine
2 eggs, separated
1 large can condensed milk
1 teaspoon grated lemon rind

Heat the lemon juice and gelatine gently until the gelatine has dissolved, Whisk the egg whites until very stiff. Whisk the egg yolks until pale. Add the gelatine mixture and the condensed milk and beat thoroughly. Fold in the stiffly beaten egg whites. Pour the mixture into the prepared pie shell and allow to set. Sprinkle with the grated lemon rind before serving.

Lemon Pie made with biscuit crust pastry.

ROUGH PUFF PASTRY

Rough puff pastry is traditionally used for sweet dishes such as mince pies, jam puffs, etc. and it is the easiest to make of the *flaky-type* pastries.

> **8 ounces (225 grams) plain flour**
> **pinch of salt**
> **6 ounces (175 grams) butter or margarine**
> **6–8 tablespoons ice-cold water**

Have ready an ungreased pie-dish, baking sheet, etc., according to the recipe used.

Preheat the oven and set to hot 425°F, 220°C or Gas Mark 7, or very hot as stated in the recipe used, 15 minutes before required.

Sieve flour and salt together into a mixing bowl. Cut fat into small pieces (size of a walnut), add to the flour, and toss lightly with the fingertips, so that each piece of fat is coated with flour, but not broken up. Add the water to the flour and fat and mix lightly with the blade of a knife, making sure that the pieces of fat are still kept whole. If some of the flour is still loose, add a little more water, a teaspoon at a time, and mix in until all the flour is worked in and the dough is fairly soft. Sprinkle the dough well with flour, and flour the board well. Gather up the dough with the finger-

Sausage Rolls made with Rough Puff Pastry.

tips, turn out onto the board, and again sprinkle with flour. Form into a small oblong with the fingertips, flour the rolling pin, and roll out to a strip about 8 by 5 inches. Fold in three by folding the bottom third of the pastry upwards and the top third downwards and over the bottom fold.

FIRST ROLLING:

With the rolling-pin, lightly press the three open edges of the pastry together to seal.
Brush off any surplus flour with a pastry brush.

Turn the pastry round on the board so that the sealed right-hand edge faces you.

Now roll out to a strip about 9 by 6 inches, using the rolling-pin lightly. Brush off the surplus flour.

SECOND ROLLING:

Again fold the pastry in three. Seal the edges. Turn round on the board so that the right-hand edge faces you. Again roll to a strip approximately 9 by 6 inches and brush off the surplus flour.

Fold in three again, seal edges and place on a floured plate. Sprinkle with flour, cover with a damp cloth and leave in a cool place (a refrigerator, if you have one) for 20 minutes.

THIRD ROLLING:

Brush off any surplus flour and repeat rolling as in second rolling.

FOURTH ROLLING:

As you did for third rolling. (Give a fifth or sixth rolling and resting but never over-roll.) After the final resting, roll out again to the thickness required and continue as directed in recipe used. Bake on the second shelf from top. Temperature hot or very hot according to recipe used. Time—see individual recipes.

SAUSAGE ROLLS

Baking time: 20–25 minutes
> **8 ounces (225 grams) rough puff or flaky pastry**
> **¾–1 pound (450 grams) sausage meat**

Preheat the oven to 450°F, 230°C or Gas Mark 8. Roll the pastry out thinly and trim off the edges. Cut long strips of pastry about 3 inches wide. Roll the sausage meat into a long even strip, the length of the pastry. Place the sausage along the centre of the pastry. Fold the pastry over and seal the edges evenly. Flake the edges with the back of a knife and cut into 2-inch pieces. Make two diagonal cuts across the top of each roll. Paint the top with beaten egg (not the flaked part). Place on a baking sheet a small distance apart. Cook on the second top shelf for 20–25 minutes.
Makes 10–12 sausage rolls.

Steak and Kidney Pie made with Flaky Pastry.

FLAKY PASTRY

Flaky pastry is a little more difficult to make than Rough Puff but it makes a light delicious pastry for pies and tarts.

8 ounces (225 grams) plain flour
6 ounces (175 grams) cooking fat, lard (or cooking fat and margarine or butter mixed)
squeeze of lemon juice
$\frac{1}{2}$ level teaspoon salt
cold water to mix

Sieve the flour and salt into a basin. Divide fat into four. Rub a quarter into the flour. Make a pliable dough with lemon juice and cold water. Knead lightly with the finger-tips to an even texture. Roll into an oblong of about $\frac{1}{4}$-inch thick. Put the second quarter of fat in small knobs evenly over two-thirds of the dough. Fold into three so that the layers of dough and fat alternate. Turn dough once to the left so that the fold is to the left hand. Roll out again into an oblong. Repeat the process twice until all the fat is used. Fold into three again. Seal edges. Leave in a cool place for at least 1 hour. The pastry is improved if it is left to rest for 15 minutes or so in a cool place between each rolling. It is a good plan to make the pastry the day before it is required.

Flaky Pastry

Step 1. Roll out the dough to a rectangle 10" x 5". Add second portion of fat in small pieces by dabbing the top two thirds of the dough keeping the fat in rows. Flour lightly. Leave ½ inch margin around the pastry.

Step 2. Fold the uncovered third of the dough upwards and the top third downwards over the bottom fold. With the rolling pin lightly press the 3 open edges together.

Step 3. Brush off any surplus flour with a pastry brush. Turn dough so that the longer sealed edge is on the left and roll out to a strip about 9" x 6". Proceed with 3rd and 4th portions of fat as in step 1, resting dough between the 2nd and 3rd rolling for about 20 minutes in the refrigerator.

STEAK AND KIDNEY PIE

Baking time: 2½ hours
- 8 ounces (225 grams) flaky pastry
- 3 tablespoons oil
- 1 pound (½ kilo.) lean stewing steak (top rump is delicious and cuts the cooking time by ½ hour)
- 6–8 ounces (200 grams) ox kidney
- 2 tablespoons seasoned flour
- 1 medium onion, peeled and finely chopped
- ¼ pint (1½ decilitres) cold water
- 1 teaspoon Worcester sauce

Cut the meat into small cubes and toss in seasoned flour. Skin, wash and dry the kidney. Cut in small pieces and toss in the flour. Heat the oil in a frying pan and fry the meat until golden brown. Add the chopped onion for about the last 2 minutes then add the water and Worcester sauce. Turn into the pie-dish and allow to cool. Preheat the oven to 425°F, 220°C or Gas Mark 7. If you prefer you can cut out this stage and simply pile up the seasoned and floured meat in the pie-dish and pour on the water.

Roll the pastry to about ¼ inch thick and at least 1 inch larger all round than the pie-dish. Brush round the rim of the pie-dish with water.

Cut off narrow strips round the edge of the pastry and line the rim of the pie-dish, pressing gently. Brush over the pastry strips with water.

Lift the round of pastry on the rolling-pin place over the pie-dish and press down gently all round the rim. Lift the pie on the palm of the left hand and trim off the pastry even with the rim.

Flake and flute the edges of the pastry.

Make a hole in the top for the steam to escape.

Roll out the remaining scraps of pastry, cut into 5 or 6 diamond shapes brush with water, and press on round the hole in the shape of a flower, with the dampened sides underneath.

Brush over the top of the pastry with beaten egg.

Bake on the third top shelf of the preheated oven for about 20–25 minutes. Cover the pie with greaseproof paper and turn the temperature down to 350°F, 175°C or Gas Mark 4 and cook for a further 1¾–2 hours.

Since it is very important that every pie should have some good gravy, the dish should be half-filled with stock or water before covering, and additional liquid poured in when the pie is cooked. When the bones and trimmings have been taken from the meat these can be used to make a little more stock whilst the pie is cooling.

Makes 6 servings.

SAUSAGE AND BACON LOAF

Baking time: 30 minutes

8 ounces (225 grams) flaky pastry
8 ounces (225 grams) sausage meat
2 ounces (50 grams) chopped bacon, fried
  lightly
½ teaspoon mixed dried herbs
or
a few leaves of mint, finely chopped
1 tablespoon parsley, finely chopped
salt and pepper
1 teaspoon Worcester sauce
1 egg, beaten

Preheat the oven to 450°F, 230°C or Gas Mark 8. Roll the flaky pastry into an oblong about 10 inches long. Place the sausage meat, herbs and seasoning in a bowl, mix together with about half of the egg. Form the mixture into a fat roll and place down the centre of the pastry leaving an equal amount of pastry round the side of the sausage. Cut the border pastry in ½ inch strips like the branches of a tree. Brush the strips with egg and plait the strips of pastry over the filling. Glaze with beaten egg. Bake on the second top shelf of a hot oven for 15 minutes then reduce the heat to 350°F, 180°C or Gas Mark 4 for a further 15–20 minutes to allow the sausage meat to cook through.

This is an excellent picnic meal and a very popular economical family supper dish.
Makes 6 portions.

VOL-AU-VENT

Baking time: 20 minutes

8 ounces (225 grams) flaky or puff pastry
1 egg, beaten

Preheat the oven to 425°F, 220°C or Gas Mark 7. Roll out the pastry (puff pastry is better if you are using the vol-au-vents for entertaining) ¼-inch thick. Use a large round biscuit cutter or a wide mouthed cup if the vol-au-vents are for a main course. A 2-inch scone cutter will provide the small party vol-au-vents. Cut a hole 1¼ inches in diameter out of half the rounds. Brush the whole rounds with egg wash and place a cut out round on top, cook the small rounds as lids. Chill for at least 20 minutes and then bake on the second top shelf for about 20 minutes; when the pastry has risen and is a golden brown colour, remove and cool on a wire rack. Remove any soft pastry from the middle. Store in an airtight tin until needed. Fill just before serving otherwise pastry will become soggy.

Fillings can be varied from left-over chicken, meat or shellfish and mushroom in a white sauce to steak and kidney. Small vol-au-vents with savoury fillings make excellent accompaniments to drinks.

JALOUSIE

Baking time: 20–25 minutes

8 ounces (225 grams) flaky pastry
2 tablespoons raspberry or
  strawberry jam or
1 can mandarin oranges
glaze (see page 70)

Preheat the oven to 425°F, 220°C or Gas Mark 7. Roll out the pastry into 2 oblong pieces 8 by 4½ inches. Place one oblong on the baking sheet, spread the raspberry or strawberry jam in the centre leaving ½ inch all round. Fold the remaining oblong over sideways and cut through the folded edge at intervals to make slits leaving a ½-inch margin. Open out the pastry. Damp the edge with water and place on top of the strip covered with jam. Press the edges to seal, brush over with water and sprinkle with caster sugar. Allow to stand in the refrigerator for 20 minutes. Bake on the second top shelf 20–25 minutes. Cool on a wire tray and serve cut into slices.

Alternatively make a longer oblong, using apricot jam. Cut remaining pastry into long strips 1 inch wide. Damp the edges and place the strips round the edge, without covering jam. Cook as above and fill with mandarin oranges when cold. Cover with a glaze, decorate with cream if desired.
Makes 8 slices.

Jalousie made with Flaky Pastry.

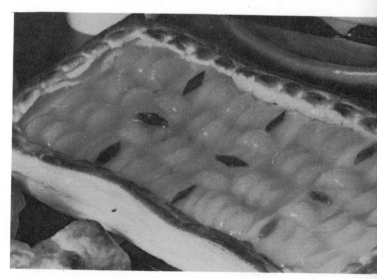

PUFF PASTRY

Baking time: see individual recipes
1 pound (450 grams) plain flour
1 teaspoon salt
1 pound (450 grams) butter or margarine
scant ½ pint (3 decilitres) water
few drops lemon juice (optional)

Sieve flour and salt into a bowl. Rub in 1 ounce (25 grams) of fat and mix with water and lemon juice to a firm dough. Soften fat by beating or moulding with the hands and form into oblong pliable cake. Roll out dough to a square about ¾-inch thick, turn onto a lightly floured marble or formica surface, and place fat in the centre. Fold dough over fat up one-third and down one-third like a parcel and wrap in greaseproof paper. Seal edges and allow to rest for 15 minutes. Put the dough on a floured surface and make four dents on the top with rolling pin to flatten pastry slightly. Roll out to three times the length with a lightly floured rolling pin. Fold up one-third, down one-third, sealing the edges with the rolling pin. Give the pastry one half turn and repeat process seven times in all. Rest in refrigerator or cool larder between every second rolling.

Use for Vol-au-vents, Mille-feuille, and fish, meat and sweet recipes which require a crust.

CHEESE SLICES

Baking time: 12 minutes
4 ounces (100 grams) puff pastry
1 egg
2 ounces (50 grams) grated cheese
salt, pepper and mustard
cayenne pepper
1 ounce (25 grams) cheese

Preheat the oven to 450°F, 230°C or Gas Mark 8. Roll the pastry thinly and divide into two portions. Beat the egg in a small bowl then add grated cheese, mustard, salt, pepper and cayenne pepper. Spread the mixture on one half of the pastry, wet the edge of the piece of pastry and place the second slice on top. Press edges together. Brush over with beaten egg. Cut into strips about 1 inch wide and 2½ inches long, sprinkle with the extra ounce of cheese. Bake on a baking sheet in the preheated oven 450°F, 230°C or Gas Mark 8 for 15 minutes then reduce heat to 375°F, 190°C or Gas Mark 5 for a further 10 minutes. Divide into fingers when cool. These can be used as a hot or cold savoury.
Makes 10 slices.

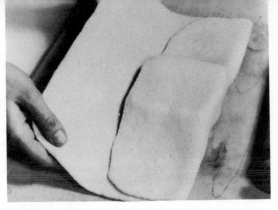

Puff Pastry.

Step 1. Turn the dough onto a formica work top or marble slab, dust with flour. Leave 2 minutes, then roll out to a square about ¾ of an inch thick. Pat or squeeze the butter to make it soft or "rollable". Form into a square cake and press into the centre of the dough. Fold and turn sides in over the butter like a parcel.

Step 2. Lightly flatten the parcel of pastry with the rolling pin and then roll out into an oblong. Fold up one third and down one third.

Step 3. After each rolling, fold the pastry into 3, keeping the rectangular shape to ensure even rolling and rising of the pastry.

MILLE FEUILLES

Baking time: 15 minutes

> **6 ounces (175 grams) puff pastry**
> **strawberry jam**
> **½ pint (3 decilitres) thick cream,**
>   **whipped**
> **1 teaspoon caster sugar**
> **chopped almonds (optional)**

Preheat the oven to 425°F, 220°C or Gas Mark 7. Roll out the pastry as thinly as possible to the size of a baking sheet and lay on a wet baking sheet. Prick well with a fork and allow to rest for at least 10 minutes. Bake the pastry in a hot oven, second top shelf for 10 minutes until golden brown.

Turn the pastry sheet over and brown underside for 5 minutes then allow to cool on a wire rack. When cool cut into 3 equal oblong strips about 3 inches wide. Crush the trimmings for the sides and, if liked, mix with browned almond flakes. Spread the first layer with jam then whipped cream. Do the same with the second layer. Spread the chopped pastry and almonds round the side and sprinkle the top with icing sugar. Cut into slices to serve.

Alternatively the top can be decorated with fruit and cream.

Makes 6 portions

Mille Feuilles made with puff pastry.

BOTERLETTERS

The 5th of December in Holland is the day when the children receive their presents as it is celebrated as the birthday of St. Nicholas. The children are often given their initials in large chocolate letters at the parties held on this day.

For the older members of the family Boterletters are made with puff pastry and almond paste and made into the initials of the family name. Try making these cut into slices or form them into initials as the Dutch do.

Baking time: 25 minutes

> **8 ounces (225 grams) puff pastry**
> FILLING:
> **1 egg, beaten**
> **5 ounces (150 grams) ground almonds**
> **3 ounces (75 grams) caster sugar**
> **2 ounces (50 grams) icing sugar**
> **1 tablespoon lemon juice**
> GLAZE:
> **1 egg, beaten**

Preheat the oven to 425°F, 220°C or Gas Mark 8. Roll out pastry to an oblong about 15 by 8 inches, trim edges and cut into 8 by 2½-inch strips. Beat egg until just frothy. Add ground almonds, sugars, lemon juice and mix to a smooth paste. Roll into long sausage shapes about ¾-inch thick.

Cut almond filling into same lengths as pastry

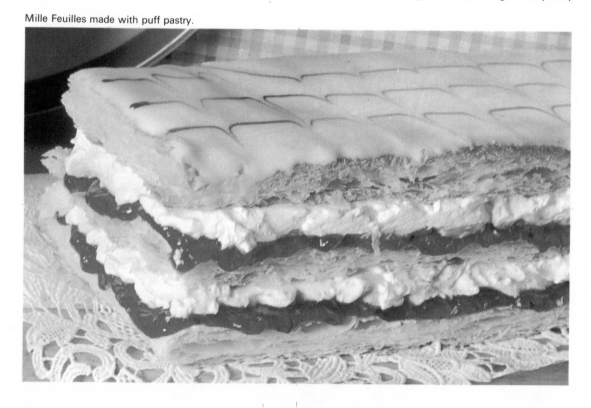

strips. Wrap pastry round filling, seal edges and ends with beaten egg. Shape into letters to represent the initial of the family name. Place on a baking sheet and brush with beaten egg. Bake in a hot oven for 25 minutes until golden brown. Cool. Makes 6 letters.

Napoleons

Baking time: 30 minutes
8 ounces (225 grams) puff pastry
TO DECORATE AND FILL:
**¼ pint (1½ decilitres) thick cream,
    whipped
glacé icing
melted chocolate**

Preheat the oven to 450°F, 230°C or Gas Mark 8. Roll the pasty into a 14 by 8-inch rectangle and about 3/8-inch thick. Cut off all the edges with a floured sharp knife. Prick the dough with a fork and cut into 3½ by 2-inch rectangles. Place on a baking sheet and cover with 3 thicknesses of damp paper towels. Put in the fridge to rest for 30 minutes. Brush evenly with slightly beaten egg white and water mixture. Bake in the preheated hot oven for 6 minutes then lower the temperature to 300°F, 150°C or Gas Mark 2 for a further 25 minutes. Cool on a wire rack.

Separate each slice into 3 layers. Sandwich together with whipped cream. Dip the top layer in glacé icing, hold above the bowl for a few minutes to allow excess to run off then place on top of second layer of cream. Make a small piping bag with greaseproof paper, spoon in the melted chocolate and pipe 2 wavy chocolate lines down the pastry slice.
Makes 8–10 slices.

Palmiers

Baking time: 15–20 minutes
**4 ounces (125 grams) puff pastry
caster sugar**

Preheat the oven to 425°F, 220°C or Gas Mark 7. Roll out the pastry on a floured board into an oblong about 8 by 14 inches. Brush lightly with cold water. Fold the narrow ends to the centre, again brush with water and fold again so that the folded edges are together. Cut into ½-inch strips with a sharp knife. Brush the cut side of each with water and sprinkle with caster sugar. Put on a baking sheet allow some space for spreading, leave in the refrigerator for about 20 minutes. Bake on the second top shelf for 15–20 minutes, turning them over halfway through the baking time to bake both sides until golden brown and crisp.
Makes 12 Palmiers.

Napoleons

SUET CRUST PASTRY

This can be used for meat and fruit puddings. If you think your family don't like this pastry—try them! At lunch-time, "pubs" in the city of London do a roaring trade with *Steak and Kidney Puddings* and *Spotted Dick*. It seems that men still enjoy these old-fashioned dishes.

    8 ounces (225 grams) plain flour
    ¼ teaspoon salt
    1 teaspoon baking powder
    3–4 ounces (100 grams) chopped or
        shredded suet
    cold water to mix

Sieve the flour, salt and baking powder into a bowl. Chop suet finely using a little flour or use shredded suet out of a packet. Add suet to the flour and mix to a firm dough with cold water. Use as required for puddings or dumplings for stew.

STEAK AND KIDNEY PUDDING

Steaming time: 3½ hours
    8 ounces (225 grams) suet crust pastry
    1 pound (½ kilo.) stewing steak
        (shoulder is ideal)
    8 ounces (225 grams) ox kidney
    2 tablespoons seasoned flour

Trim the meat removing skin and fat and cut into *small* cubes. Dip in seasoned flour. Roll out pastry (reserve one-third of the pastry for the top) into a round about ¼-inch thick and line a greased pudding basin. Press well into the basin to make sure there are no creases. Put the meat into a bowl with the pastry and add about 3–4 tablespoons of stock or water.

Roll out the pastry for the lid, damp the edges, place the lid on top and press the edges together with your hands. Cover with greased greaseproof paper if the pudding is going to be steamed or with a pudding cloth if it is to be boiled. For a really good suet pudding it is worth while using a pudding cloth because the water tends to get in with paper or foil. Tie the cloth tightly with a piece of string under the rim of the basin and allow a pleat or fold in the cloth over the centre of the pudding to allow for rising. Place the pudding in a large saucepan of boiling water and steam for about 3½ hours. Try to keep the water boiling all the time and always add boiling water to replace the water which has evaporated. Serve from a pudding basin or turn out onto hot serving dish.

Note for those who like garlic: cut a clove of garlic in two and rub the inside of the pudding basin well with it before lining the basin with pastry. Another extra you might like to try is sliced mushrooms popped into the lined basin along with the meat.
Makes 6 servings.

APPLE DUMPLING

Steaming time: 3 hours
    8 ounces (225 grams) suet crust pastry
    3–4 cooking apples
    3 ounces (75 grams) soft brown sugar

Roll out the pastry and line a pudding basin as for steak and kidney pudding. Peel and core apples then cut in thick slices and add alternate layers of apples and sugar into the pudding basin. Roll out the pastry for the lid, damp the edges and place the lid on top. Press the edges firmly together to ensure a good seal. Cover with a pudding cloth, allowing enough material for a pleat on top to allow the dumpling to rise. Tie the cloth tightly with a string under the rim of the basin. Place the pudding in a large saucepan of boiling water and allow to cook for about 3 hours. Keep the water boiling all the time by adding boiling water to replace the water which has boiled away.

Delicious served with fresh cream or a custard sauce.
Makes 6 servings.

VARIATION:
Divide the suet crust pastry into 4. Put a whole peeled and cored apple in the centre of each portion of pastry. Fill the core with brown sugar. Cover the apple with the suet pastry damping the edges to join them firmly together. Tie each apple dumpling in pudding cloth, boil gently for about 2 hours.
Makes 2 servings from each apple unless the apples are small.

Apple Dumpling made with suet pastry.

HOT WATER CRUST PASTRY ✓

This pastry can be used for making raised pies such as veal and ham pie, pork pie or game pie. This is mixed using hot water and so should be moulded while warm and pliable either into the pie shape using the hands or into a special pie mould (open at the side so as to be removed easily when the pie is cooked).

> 1 pound (450 grams) plain flour
> 6 ounces (175 grams) lard
> 1 teaspoon salt
> ¼ pint (1½ decilitres) milk or water

Add the lard to the milk or water and bring to the boil in a small saucepan. Then add the flour sieved with the salt. Use a wooden spoon to beat into a stiff mixture. Knead well on a wooden board and keep warm.

VEAL AND HAM PIE

Baking time: 2 hours 50 minutes
> 1 pound (450 grams) hot water
>   crust pastry
FILLING:
> 1½ pounds (½ kilo.) lean veal
> 8 ounces (225 grams) gammon
> pinch of pepper
> 1 teaspoon salt
> grated rind of ½ lemon
> 1 tablespoon parsley, chopped
> 2 eggs, hardboiled
> ¼ pint (1½ decilitres) stock
> 1 dessertspoon gelatine
> beaten egg
> milk

Preheat the oven to 400°F, 200°C or Gas Mark 6. Make pastry as in pastry recipe. Cut the veal and ham into small pieces, make sure any pieces of fat are removed. Mix with the seasoning, lemon rind and parsley. Thoroughly grease a raised pie mould or mould the pastry in a cake tin and put it on a greased baking tray.

Set aside part of the pastry for the lid and roll out the rest to a ½-inch thickness. Line the bottom of the mould with the pastry and knead well with the knuckles from the centre to the edges to remove any air. Line the sides of the tin pressing the pastry well in with the thumbs. See that the pastry overlaps the top of the rim. Take half of the filling and pack in well, place the eggs along the middle and cover with remaining filling. Roll out pasty lid and place it on top after damping edges of the pie. Press edges firmly and trim. Make a small hole in the centre of the top, brush with beaten egg and milk, and arrange small leaves of pastry on top as a decoration.

Cook in the centre of a hot oven, 400°C or Gas Mark 6, for 20 minutes and then 350°F or Gas Mark 4 for a further 2½ hours. Make the pastry a shiny brown by occasionally brushing with beaten egg and milk during the baking.

After the pie has been in the oven for 1½ hours, remove the mould, brush again with egg and milk, and return to the oven.

After the pie has cooled, pour jellied stock through the hole.

A well-seasoned stock may be made from the bones and trimmings of the veal, with a little gelatine added if necessary.

Makes 6–8 servings.

MUTTON PIES

Baking time: 30–40 minutes
- **1 pound (450 grams)**
  hot water crust pastry
- **12 ounces (350 grams) lean mutton**
- **1 small onion**
- **1 teaspoon chopped parsley**
- **½ teaspoon thyme**
- **salt and pepper**
- **1–2 tablespoons stock or water**
- **2 teaspoons Worcester sauce**

Preheat the oven to 350°F, 180°C or Gas Mark 4. Prepare the mutton by removing fat, bone and gristle. Chop the meat into small pieces add the chopped onion and mix with the herbs and seasoning. Turn the pastry onto a floured board and knead until free from cracks. Keep one third of the pastry warm and divide the remainder into six pieces. With this pastry line six small ring moulds or mould the pastry round a tumbler or other suitable shape. These little pies are round and have straight sides but one can improvise. Fill the pastry with seasoned mutton mixture and moisten both edges firmly together. Trim with a pair of kitchen scissors. Make a hole in the centre of each pie and brush with a little milk or beaten egg. Bake in a moderate oven for 30–40 minutes, remove from tins or rings and fill with hot gravy or stock. Serve piping hot.

Makes 6 pies.

Veal and Ham Pie made with Hot Water Crust Pastry.

CHOUX PASTRY

Sweetened and shaped with a pastry tube this pastry can be combined with a variety of delightful fillings. The pastry is made by heating the fat and water in a saucepan and when it has reached boiling point the sieved plain flour is tipped in and the paste is beaten until smooth. This stage should only last a few seconds as prolonged beating may result in badly risen choux pastry. The pastry may be beaten thoroughly after the eggs are added. Bake on a baking sheet which has been run under the cold tap for a few minutes. When filling the baked pastry remember that cream-based and egg-based fillings must be kept cool or refrigrated. Fill as close to serving time as possible to avoid sogginess. Whipped or flavoured cream, custard, chocolate or coffee fillings, or else ice cream all make delicious fillings.

Baking time: 40 minutes
  $\frac{1}{2}$ pint ($2\frac{1}{2}$ decilitres) water
  5 ounces (125 grams) butter
  5 ounces (125 grams) plain flour
  pinch of salt
  3 eggs

Preheat the oven to 400°F, 200°C or Gas Mark 6. Heat water and butter in a saucepan. When the water bubbles, add the sieved flour. Remove from the heat and beat immediately. Beat hard until mixture leaves the side of the pan. Allow mixture to cool and beat in the eggs gradually. Pipe on to a greased sheet, either in 3-inch lengths for éclair shapes or in rounds for cream buns. Bake in a hot oven for about 30 minutes. Make a slit in each and return to the oven to dry for 5–10 minutes.
Note: It is better to make choux pastry only a few hours before using it otherwise it can be leathery.
Makes 8–12 depending on size.

1. Add the butter or margarine to boiling water in a saucepan. Stir with a wooden spoon till butter melts. Add sieved flour and salt all at once and stir vigorously.

2. Cook and stir till dough pulls away from sides of pan and forms a ball around spoon. Remove from heat; vigorously beat in eggs, one at a time.

3. Pipe or drop tablespoonfuls or teaspoonfuls of dough on to a greased sheet. Bake, split the puffs or éclairs; turn off heat, allow to dry in oven 10 minutes. Cool on a wire tray.

PROFITEROLES

Baking time: 20–30 minutes
   1 quantity choux pastry
   confectioner's custard (see page 58)
   CHOCOLATE SAUCE:
   6 ounces (175 grams) dark chocolate
   ½ pint (3 decilitres) water
   4 ounces (125 grams) granulated sugar

Preheat the oven to 400°F, 200°C or Gas Mark 6. Make the Choux Pastry. Place teaspoons of mixture on a dampened baking sheet. Bake for 20–30 minutes until crisp. Slit each ball to allow the steam to escape. Allow to cool. Break up the chocolate for the sauce and melt in a pan with water over a low heat. When melted and smooth add the sugar. Allow the sugar to dissolve, bring to the boil and simmer for 15 minutes until the sauce is a coating consistency. Watch it carefully to prevent burning. Fill the buns with confectioner's custard or whipped fresh cream. Pile up in a pyramid and pour the chocolate sauce over the pyramid allowing it to drip on to the bottom buns.

For a special dinner party sweet I often use spun sugar to decorate. Use half the Caramel Topping quantity on page 89 and add a pinch of cream of tartar. When the caramel reaches soft ball stage when dropped in cold water, or a 6-inch thread is obtained, then the sugar is ready. Place two wooden spoons or rolling pins on the floor or table with greaseproof paper underneath and using a clean new wire brush (one that looks like a garden broom or make one yourself with fuse wire) spin the sugar back and forwards over the two wooden handles. Spun sugar will last about 20 minutes on a soft sweet or will remain crisp about 2 hours on its own.

SAVOURY CHOUX FLAN

Baking time: 40 minutes
   1 quantity of choux pastry
FILLING:
   2 ounces (50 grams) flour
   2 ounces (50 grams) butter
   1 pint (6 decilitres) milk
   salt and pepper
   2 ounces (50 grams) mushrooms, chopped
   1 can tuna fish

   2 tomatoes
   several sprigs of parsley

Preheat the oven to 425°F, 220°C or Gas Mark 7. Make up the Choux Pastry and fill a piping bag with a plain pipe. Starting in the centre of a greased baking sheet, pipe round until a shape like a catherine wheel is formed. Pipe complete circle as an outside wall. Place on the top shelf in a preheated oven for about 25 minutes, then place on a lower shelf to continue cooking for the remaining time. Make the white sauce by stirring the butter and flour together in a saucepan over a low heat. Stir in the milk gradually, bring to the boil and stir until a smooth sauce is obtained. Season well. Add finely chopped mushrooms, flaked tuna fish, and tip the hot filling into the hot choux flan as it comes out of the oven. Garnish with tomatoes and parsley. Makes 4 servings.

ALTERNATIVE FILLINGS:

Chicken and Ham

Increase the mushrooms to 4 ounces. Use about 8 ounces chopped chicken in place of the tuna fish.

Egg and Cheese

Omit the mushrooms and tuna fish. Stir 4 ounces finely grated Cheddar cheese and 2 chopped hard-boiled eggs into the sauce. Add a pinch of dry mustard with the salt and pepper.

Cheese and Asparagus

Omit the mushrooms and tuna fish. Stir 2 ounces finely grated Cheddar cheese and well drained and chopped canned asparagus spears into the sauce.

COCKTAIL CHOUX BUNS

   1 quantity of choux pastry
   Filling:
   Cream cheese flavoured with chopped chives

Pre-heat oven to 400°F (200°C) or Gas Mark 6. Make the choux pastry. Place teaspoon of mixture on a dampened baking sheet and bake for 20–30 minutes until crisp. Slit each bun to allow steam to escape. Allow to cool on a wire tray. Fill the buns with the chive-flavoured cream cheese sprinkled with paprika pepper.
   In place of cream cheese as a filling you could use any of the fillings suggested for the savoury Choux Flan.

FRIED CHOUX PASTRY
Sweet Beignets

Cooking time: 8 minutes approximately

1 quantity choux pastry
Serve with :
heated jam or lemon curd
caster sugar

Make up the Choux Pastry, retaining half of the second egg to ensure the paste is firm, as described on page 84. Place teaspoons of mixture on a baking sheet. Heat a pan of deep fat or oil until a cube of bread turns golden brown when dropped into the pan. Lift the paste into the fat with an oiled palette knife. Allow lots of room for the paste to rise. Too many at once will cool the fat and give a soggy result. Cook for about eight minutes or until golden brown. Lift out of the pan onto kitchen paper to drain. Dredge with caster sugar and serve with heated jam or lemon curd.

Cheese Beignets

Cooking time: 8 minutes

1 quantity choux pastry
2 tablespoons grated Cheddar cheese
2 tablespoons grated Parmesan cheese
cayenne pepper

Make the pastry and add 2 tablespoons grated Cheddar cheese. Cook as for Sweet Beignets but after draining sprinkle with grated cheese and cayenne pepper. These make delicious cocktail savouries if you can bear the smell of frying near party time !

Choux Buns with Chocolate
and Walnut Topping

REGIONAL & CONTINENTAL CAKES

GATEAU AUX FRAMBOISES

Baking time: 40–45 minutes
  6 ounces (175 grams) plain flour
  1 tablespoon soft brown sugar
  6 ounces (175 grams) soft butter
  1 tablespoon raspberry jam
TOPPING:
  fresh raspberries
  whipped cream or
  dredged icing sugar

Preheat the oven to 325°F, 170°C or Gas Mark 3. Sieve the flour into a mixing bowl, then add the sugar and butter. Mix and knead together until it forms a smooth mixture. Turn out on to a well-floured board. Divide into four equal portions. Roll each thinly into a round and trim off the edges with a 6-inch saucepan lid used as a cutter. Roll out the trimmings into a round and cut into shape as before. Carefully lift the rounds onto two baking sheets and prick with a fork. Bake in a pre-heated very moderate oven on middle shelf for 40–45 minutes. Leave to cool slightly on baking sheet for 2–3 minutes. Heat the raspberry jam in a saucepan. Lift one round on to a warm serving dish and spread with hot jam; continue to layer the remaining rounds on top with more jam, but leave the top one plain and dredge with icing sugar (for an attractive top, dredge the sugar through a fancy doiley).

Alternatively, spread the top layer with whipped cream and add raspberries just before serving. Makes 6 portions.

MOCHA GATEAU

Baking time : 20 minutes
  6 ounces (175 grams) margarine
  6 ounces (175 grams) caster sugar
  1 tablespoon cocoa and 1 dessertspoon instant coffee, blended with 2 table-spoons warm water
  3 eggs
  6 ounces (175 grams) self-raising flour

Preheat the oven to 350°F, 177°C or Gas Mark 4. Cream the fat to a light fluffy texture. Add the coffee and cocoa mixture and continue to cream. When it is well blended, add the eggs one by one with a tablespoon of self-raising flour with the last egg. Sieve in the remaining flour and fold in with a tablespoon. Bake in two 7-inch sandwich tins in the preheated oven.

ICING
  2 ounces (50 grams) margarine or butter
  8 ounces (225 grams) icing sugar
  1 tablespoon cocoa
  1 dessertspoon instant coffee, blended with 2 tablespoons milk
  6 whole walnuts
  chopped walnuts

Cream the margarine with a little icing sugar until soft and fluffy. Add the cocoa and coffee mixture with the remaining icing sugar and mix thoroughly.

After the cake has cooled, spread icing in the middle and round the sides. Roll the sides of the cake in chopped walnuts. Spread remaining cream icing on top.
Decorate with 6 walnuts.

ALMOND TORTE

Baking time: 45 minutes
  6 eggs
  6 ounces (150 grams) caster sugar
  4 ounces (100 grams) ground almonds
  2 ounces (50 grams) plain flour

Preheat the oven to 375°F, 190°C or Gas Mark 5. Grease an 8-9-inch cake tin. Separate the eggs. Beat the whites until stiff and peaky, add the sugar beat for another minute then add the yolks beating in one at a time. Beat well for another 1–2 minutes. Sieve the flour and almonds together and fold into the egg mixture. Turn into the cake tin and bake for 45 minutes. Serve plain, sprinkled with icing sugar, or fill with whipped cream and fruit.

PEAR AND ALMOND KUGELHOPF

Baking time: 45–50 minutes
  2 pears, peeled, cored and diced
  juice ½ lemon
  4 ounces (125 grams) butter
  4 ounces (125 grams) sugar
  2 eggs
  2 ounces (50 grams) treacle
  7 ounces (200 grams) plain flour
  2 tablespoons ground almonds
  1 teaspoon ginger
  1 teaspoon mixed spice
  1 teaspoon bicarbonate of soda
  ½ pint (3 decilitres) milk

Preheat the oven to 375°F, 200°C or Gas Mark 5. Marinate diced pear in lemon juice. Cream butter and sugar, gradually beat in the eggs. Stir in the treacle. Sieve remaining dry ingredients. Add the warm milk to the bicarbonate of soda and add alternately, to the creamed mixture, along with the dry ingredients. Lastly fold in the diced pear. Grease a kugelhopf mould and fill with the mixture. Bake in a moderate oven for 45–50 minutes. Leave 5 minutes before unmoulding. Serve either hot or cold, dredged with icing sugar. Makes 6 servings.

SAFFRON CAKE

Baking time: 1¼ hours
  ¼ teaspoon powdered saffron
  7 tablespoons water
  1 ounce (25 grams) fresh yeast
  1 tablespoon sugar
  12 ounces (325 grams) plain flour
  ¼ teaspoon salt
  ¼ teaspoon mixed spice
  8 ounces (200 grams) butter or
      margarine
  4 ounces (100 grams) mixed peel
  8 ounces (200 grams) currants

1: With dried yeast, use approximately one-third the quantity of fresh yeast.
2: If saffron is bought in thread form, powder before use.
  Place the saffron in a cup or jug of the water and place in a saucepan of warm water until it becomes lukewarm. Cream the yeast and then add the saffron water. Sieve the flour, salt, mixed spice and sugar, make a well in the centre then pour in the yeast mixture. Mix thoroughly and cover the bowl with a polythene bag. Allow to stand in a warm, draught-free place for 20 minutes. Do not put the bowl into a low oven or you will kill the action of the yeast. Allow the fat to soften but not into an oil. Add 1 teaspoon of sugar. Gradually add to the batter, beating as you go. When it is quite smooth, add the currants and peel. Cover and set aside for 1 hour in a warm place to rise.
  Turn the dough onto a floured board and knead lightly. Put in a greased 1-pound loaf tin, cover and allow to rise for a further 20 minutes. Bake in the middle shelf of a moderate oven, 350°F, 180°C or Gas Mark 4, for 1¼ hours. Turn out and allow to cool. Spread the cake with butter for a real tea-time treat.

DORSET APPLE CAKE

Baking time: 45 minutes
  4 ounces (120 grams) self-raising flour
  2 large cooking apples, finely chopped
  1½ ounces (40 grams) suet
  2 ounces (60 grams) caster sugar
  1 egg
  2–3 tablespoons milk
TOPPING:
  2 tablespoons soft brown sugar
  1 ounce (30 grams) butter
  1 apple, peeled and cut into thin slices

To make the topping put the brown sugar and butter into a saucepan and stir until the butter is worked into the sugar but not melted. Place this mixture on the bottom of a deep 7-inch cake tin which has been greased. Arrange sliced apples in rings on top of the sugar mixture. Sieve the flour into a bowl. Add the sugar and suet. Add the egg and milk to the flour; mix in the finely chopped apples. Turn the mixture into the tin and bake in a moderate oven, 350°F, 180°C or Gas Mark 4, for about 45 minutes. Turn out so that the sliced apples top the cake.
  Delicious as a pudding served with fresh cream.

DOBOS TORTE

Baking time: about 6 minutes
  4 eggs
  6 ounces (175 grams) caster sugar
  5 ounces (150 grams) plain flour

CHOCOLATE BUTTER CREAM:
  8 ounces (225 grams) icing sugar,
    sieved
  2 ounces (60 grams) butter
  4 ounces (120 grams) dark chocolate,
    melted
CARAMEL
  5 ounces (150 grams) lump sugar
  ¼ pint (1½ decilitres) water
DECORATION:
  grated chocolate for the sides

You will need to use six baking sheets to bake this cake in the original way. Therefore, if you only have 2, re-use the sheets by brushing with oil and dusting lightly with flour between each baking. Preheat the oven to 375°F, 190°C or Gas Mark 5. Mark 8-inch rounds on greaseproof paper then oil the paper. Break the eggs into the top of a double boiler, add the sugar and beat until thick and creamy over hot water. Remove the eggs from the heat and continue beating until cold. Sieve the flour and salt then fold into the egg mixture with a metal spoon. Divide the mixture into 6 portions and pour on to each circle of oiled paper then bake in the preheated oven for 5–6 minutes. Trim round with a sharp knife and put on a wire tray to cool. Take one of the rounds and put it on a oiled baking sheet ready for a caramel topping. Sandwich the remaining five layers with chocolate butter cream. To make the caramel, melt the sugar in the water over a very low heat without boiling. Once the sugar is dissolved turn the heat up and cook until the caramel is a good brown colour. Pour this at once over the top layer which you have ready on the baking sheet. Just before the caramel has set divide into portions with an oiled knife. Trim the edges and place on top of the other five rings. Spread the sides with more chocolate butter cream and roll in grated chocolate, chopped walnuts or the remainder of the caramel, crushed. Decorate the top of the caramel with butter cream if desired.
Makes 1 cake.

QUICK DOBOS TORTE

Should the thought of making all the layers separately horrify you, try a quick torte as shown here and on page 90. Make a deep whisked sponge (see page 48) and cut into layers, sandwich together with chocolate butter cream and if the caramel topping does not appeal then use more butter icing for the top.

This is the delicious Dobos Torte, originally from Hungary. It is as rich and delicious as it looks. Torten have reached us from central Europe and are firm layer cakes with soft fillings, often eaten in their country of origin at morning or afternoon coffee, but are excellent at any time!

Dobos Torte.

FREEZING

If you have a baking day and a deep freeze you cannot do better than to make double quantities when you bake so that you have some for future use. This is a fantastic saving in time and labour for washing up. I think that more people will bake as deep freezing becomes more popular. If your need is half a cake then freeze the other half rather than have it moulding in a tin to eventually feed the birds, as I have often done in the past when the children are away from home.

BREAD

Bread can be frozen unbaked or baked to suit your convenience. Storage time depends on the type of dough and the type of baked bread. Risen dough will keep for 2–3 weeks; unrisen white for 8 weeks. Richer unrisen doughs keep for a shorter time.

UNRISEN DOUGH

Prepare the dough until the kneading stage is reached then place in a large oiled polythene bag. Seal tightly allowing for a little rising before dough is frozen.

RISEN DOUGH

Allow dough to rise for the full rising time, it should spring back when pressed lightly with the finger. Knock back the dough as described in bread making, page 9. Place in an oiled bag, seal tightly and freeze immediately.

BAKED BREAD

Freeze freshly baked bread in an ungreased polythene bag. Most bread will keep for up to 4 weeks. Crusty bread, however will only keep well for 1 week as the crust tends to break off.

BISCUITS

Cooked biscuits store well in an airtight tin, therefore there is no point in taking up valuable storage space with biscuits. However uncooked biscuit mixture, especially the rich mixtures freeze well.

CAKES

As I mentioned before, the freezer is ideal for cakes. They can be frozen plain or already iced or frosted. You can divide the cakes into portions which means you need not thaw a whole cake if you only need 3 portions. Do not wrap soft icing as it will stick and spoil the look of the cake when used. Harden icing off by freezing unwrapped for a short time then remove and wrap in the usual way. Cakes will keep 4–6 months baked; 8–10 unbaked.

Wrapping Chocolate Layer Cake for Freezing

PASTRY

Pies can be frozen baked or raw. If you are freezing covered pies, uncooked, then do not cut vents in the top until you are ready to cook as the fillings tend to dry out. Custard pies, soft milky fillings and meringue tops are not suitable for freezing. Pastry can be baked unthawed if it requires no further handling.

Pies will keep about 4 months when baked and 6 months unbaked.

Packing a Filled Flan for Freezing

Notes on Metrication

The changeover to the metric system will not be completed until 1975, however it is essential that we all become familiar with this system. The children are already using metric weights and measures in some schools. I have included the metric measurements in brackets in the recipes in this book to help you to become familiar with them gradually. It is not practical on the whole to convert one imperial measure directly into a metric one, therefore I have balanced the recipe taking the grams to the nearest 25 unit, where possible, to ensure making the correct quantity for the tin mentioned in the recipe.

Note that the word grammes has been abbreviated in this book to grams but can now in accordance with the Metrication Board also be abbreviated to g.

WEIGHT

Imperial (ounces)	Metric (grams)	Approx. Metric Measurement to Nearest 25 gram Unit
1	28·35	25
2	56·7	50
3	85·05	75
4	113·4	125
5	141·75	150
6	170·1	175
7	198·45	200
8	226.8	225
12	340·2	350
16	453·6	450
2·2 pounds	1000	1 Kilogram

CAPACITY

Imperial (pints)	Equivalent millilitres to nearest 25 ml unit	Decilitres (Approx.)
$\frac{1}{4}$	150	$1\frac{1}{2}$
$\frac{1}{2}$	275	3
$\frac{3}{4}$	425	$4\frac{1}{2}$
1	575	6
$1\frac{1}{4}$	725	$7\frac{1}{2}$
$1\frac{1}{2}$	875	9
$1\frac{3}{4}$	1000	10 = 1 litre
2		1 generous litre
$2\frac{1}{2}$		$1\frac{1}{4}$ litres
$3\frac{1}{2}$		2 litres
4		$2\frac{1}{4}$ litres

LENGTH:

1 inch = 2·54 centimetres

6 inches = 15·2 centimetres

39·37 inches = 100 centimetres = 1 metre

Oven Temperatures

Electric cooker manufacturers have recently discussed proposals for Celsius Scale markings for oven thermostats which may be introduced around 1973. The electrical manufacturers have decided to use the following markings on new ovens.

Present Electric Scale	Gas Marks	Suggested Celsius Scale
225°F	$\frac{1}{4}$	110°C
250°F	$\frac{1}{2}$	130°C
275°F	1	140°C
300°F	2	150°C
325°F	3	170°C
350°F	4	180°C
375°F	5	190°C
400°F	6	200°C
425°F	7	220°C
450°F	8	230°C
475°F	9	240°C

Index

it tars good

BASIC METHODS OF COOKING

BAKING—cooking in dry heat in the oven.

BOILING—cooking food in a boiling liquid (212°F), eg. vegetables, pasta and boiled puddings.

BRAISING—meat is browned then cooked slowly on a bed of vegetables with very little liquid, in a covered container.

FRYING—Shallow frying is cooking in just enough fat to cover the base of the pan. It is a quick method of cooking.
Deep frying is cooking food by immersing in a deep pan filled two-thirds full of hot fat or oil.

GRILLING—always pre-heat the grill for this method of cooking and brush the grill rack with fat. Food which is to be completely cooked by grilling should be cooked at a high temperature for the initial browning period. Then reduce the heat and complete the cooking.

POACHING—cooking food gently in liquid at simmering temperature (185-200°F).

POT ROASTING—a combination of frying and steaming. The meat is browned and then cooked in a heavy covered casserole or saucepan with fat only. It is a slow method of roasting and may be carried out on top of the stove or in the oven at a low temperature.

PRESSURE COOKING—cooking food at a very high temperature under pressure. The food cooks quickly and tougher types of meat are made more tender. Types of pressure cookers vary and the makers instructions should be followed explicitly.

ROASTING—cooking food at a high temperature in the oven. The container is open and little fat should be used.

SAUTÉ—To cook over a strong heat in a small amount of fat or oil, shaking the pan frequently to prevent sticking.

SIMMERING—cooking below boiling point—the liquid should bubble gently at the side of the pot.

STEAMING—using the steam from boiling water to cook food. The food may be cooked in a steamer over boiling water or the basin of food may be stood in the boiling water. Always cover the saucepan or steamer.

STEWING—cooking food at simmering point or below in a liquid. It is a long slow method of cooking and an excellent way of tenderising the tougher cuts of meat. Stewing is carried out in a covered container.

COOKING TERMS

BAIN MARIE—a roasting tin half filled with water in which a dish of food which must be baked slowly is placed before cooking in the oven, e.g. caramel custards.

BAKING BLIND—the method of baking flans, tarts and other pastry cases without a filling. Put the flan ring or pie dish on a baking sheet and line with pastry. Cut a circle of greaseproof paper slightly larger than the flan. Fill with dried beans, rice, or bread crusts to weigh the paper down. Bake the flan for 15 minutes. Remove the greaseproof paper and beans and bake a further 10 minutes to brown and crisp the pastry. Cool.

BASTING—spooning the cooking fat and liquid over food while roasting. This keeps the food moist, adds flavour and improves the appearance.

BEATING—method of introducing air to a mixture, a wooden spoon, wire whisk or electric beater may be used for this process.

BINDING—adding a liquid, egg or melted fat to a dry mixture to hold it together, e.g. beaten egg is added to mince for hamburgers.

BLANCHING—putting food in boiling water in order to either whiten, remove the skin, salt or strong flavour from food.

BLENDING—the process of mixing a thickening agent, such as flour or cornflour with a little cold water to a smooth paste. A little of the hot liquid to be thickened is then added to the paste and the whole returned to the saucepan. The mixture is stirred until it boils and thickens. Used to thicken the liquid of casseroles, stews and certain sauces.

BOUQUET GARNI—a bunch of fresh mixed herbs tied together with string and used for flavouring. Usually a bay leaf, sprig of parsley, sprig of thyme and perhaps a few celery leaves. Dried herbs may be used tied in a little muslin bag.

BROWNING—putting a cooked dish or meringue under the grill, or in the oven for a short time to give it an appetising golden colour.

CASSEROLE—baking dish usually ovenproof earthenware, pottery, porcelain or cast-iron with a tight fitting lid. Food cooked in a casserole is served straight from the dish.

CHINING—method of preparing neck or loin joints for easier carving. The bone at the wide end of the chops or cutlets is cut away from the meat so that it may be carved into portions of one rib each.

CHOPPING—dividing food into very small pieces on a chopping board using a very sharp knife.

COATING—covering food with a thin layer of flour, egg, breadcrumbs or batter before it is fried.

CONSISTENCY—term describing the texture (usually the thickness) of a mixture.

CREAMING—beating together fat and sugar to incorporate air, break down the sugar crystals and soften the fat.

FOLDING IN—to incorporate two mixtures using a light over and over motion. Usually applied to light mixtures such as whisked egg white or cream which have to be folded into other ingredients. It is important to carry out the process carefully so that the air is not knocked out of the light mixture. Flour is sifted over whisked egg mixtures for very light sponge cakes. The use of an electric mixer is not practical for this process. A sharp edged metal spoon is ideal for folding in.

GLAZE—a liquid brushed over the surface of a dish to give it a shiny finish.

GRATE—shaving food into shreds.

HULL—remove stalks from soft fruits—strawberries, raspberries etc.

KNEADING—working a dough using the fingertips for pastry-making and the knuckles for bread-making. The edges of the dough are drawn to the centre.

MARINADE—a liquid made of oil and wine, vinegar or lemon juice and flavouring vegetables, herbs and spices. Food is steeped in the marinade to tenderise and add flavour.

PURÉE—fresh or cooked fruit or vegetables are broken down into a smooth pulp by sieving, pounding or blending in the liquidiser.

REDUCING—boiling a liquid, uncovered, in order to evaporate the water content and make the liquid more concentrated.

ROUX—a thickening agent for soups and sauces. Equal quantities of fat and flour are cooked together.

RUBBING IN—a method of incorporating fat into flour, e.g. in short-crust pastry making. Add the fat in small pieces to the flour. Using the fingertips, quickly and lightly rub the fat into the flour, lifting the hands as you do this.

SEASONED FLOUR—mix 1 teaspoon of salt, a good sprinkling of pepper and 2 tablespoons flour. Use to coat food before cooking.

SIEVING—to rub food through a sieve using a wooden spoon, in order to discard skin, stalks or seeds.

SKIMMING—to remove the scum or fat from food whilst it is cooking. A piece of absorbent kitchen paper or a metal spoon are used.

STOCK—a well-flavoured liquid made by simmering meat and/or vegetables in water for a prolonged period, to extract the flavour. When time is short the commercial stock cubes may be substituted.

SWEATING—cooking foods, usually vegetables in a small amount of fat to soften and add flavour. The pan is always covered.

WATER BATH—see Bain marie.

WHIPPING OR WHISKING—adding air quickly to a mixture by beating with a hand whisk, rotary beater or electric beater.

ZEST—the thin coloured skin of citrus fruit which contains the oil and flavour.

WEIGHT EQUIVALENTS

Avoirdupois	Metric
1 ounce	= 28·35 grammes
1 pound	= 453·6 grammes
2·3 pounds	= 1 kilogram

LIQUID MEASUREMENTS

¼ pint	= 1½ decilitres
½ pint	= ¼ litre
scant 1 pint	= ½ litre
1¾ pints	= 1 litre
1 gallon	= 4·5 litres

HANDY LIQUID MEASURES

1 pint	= 20 fluid ounces	= 32 tablespoons
½ pint	= 10 fluid ounces	= 16 tablespoons
¼ pint	= 5 fluid ounces	= 8 tablespoons
⅛ pint	= 2½ fluid ounces	= 4 tablespoons
1/16 pint	= 1¼ fluid ounces	= 2 tablespoons

HANDY SOLID MEASURES

			Approximate
Almonds, ground	1 oz.	=	3¾ level tablespoons
Arrowroot	1 oz.	=	4 level tablespoons
Breadcrumbs fresh	1 oz.	=	7 level tablespoons
dried	1 oz.	=	3¼ level tablespoons
Butter and Lard	1 oz.	=	2 level tablespoons
Cheese, grated	1 oz.	=	3½ level tablespoons
Chocolate, grated	1 oz.	=	3 level tablespoons
Cocoa	1 oz.	=	2¾ level tablespoons
Dessicated Coconut	1 oz.	=	4½ tablespoons
Coffee—Instant	1 oz.	=	6 tablespoons
Ground	1 oz.	=	4 tablespoons
Cornflour	1 oz.	=	2½ tablespoons
Custard powder	1 oz.	=	2½ tablespoons
Curry Powder and Spices	1 oz.	=	5 tablespoons
Flour	1 oz.	=	4 tablespoons
Gelatine, powdered	1 oz.	=	2½ tablespoons
Rice, uncooked	1 oz.	=	·1½ tablespoons
Sugar, caster and granulated	1 oz.	=	2 tablespoons
Icing sugar	1 oz.	=	2½ tablespoons
Syrup	1 oz.	=	1 tablespoon
Yeast, granulated	1 oz.	=	1½ tablespoons

AMERICAN MEASURES

16 fluid ounces	=	1 American pint
8 fluid ounces	=	1 American standard cup
0·50 fluid ounces	=	1 American tablespoon *(slightly smaller than British Standards Institute tablespoon)*
0·16 fluid ounces	=	1 American teaspoon

AUSTRALIAN MEASURES
(Cup, Spoon and Liquid Measures)

These are the measures in everyday use in the Australian family kitchen. The spoon measures listed below are from the ordinary household cutlery set.

CUP MEASURES

(Using the 8-liquid-ounce cup measure)

1 cup flour	4 oz.
1 cup sugar *(crystal or caster)*	8 oz.
1 cup icing sugar *(free from lumps)*	5 oz.
1 cup shortening *(butter, margarine, etc.)*	8 oz.
1 cup honey, golden syrup, treacle	10 oz.
1 cup brown sugar *(lightly packed)*	4 oz.
1 cup brown sugar *(tightly packed)*	5 oz.
1 cup soft breadcrumbs	2 oz.
1 cup dry breadcrumbs *(made from fresh breadcrumbs)*	3 oz.
1 cup packet dry breadcrumbs	4 oz.
1 cup rice *(uncooked)*	6 oz.
1 cup rice *(cooked)*	5 oz.
1 cup mixed fruit or individual fruit such as sultanas, etc.	4 oz.
1 cup grated cheese	4 oz.
1 cup nuts *(chopped)*	4 oz.
1 cup coconut	2½ oz.

SPOON MEASURES

	Level Tablespoon
1 oz. Flour	2
1 oz. sugar *(crystal or caster)*	1½
1 oz. icing sugar *(free from lumps)*	2
1 oz. shortening	1
1 oz. honey	1
1 oz. gelatine	2
1 oz. cocoa	3
1 oz. cornflour	2½
1 oz. custard powder	2½

LIQUID MEASURES

(Using 8-liquid-ounce cup)

1 cup liquid	8 oz
2½ cups liquid	20 oz. (1 pint)
2 tablespoons liquid	1 oz.
1 gill liquid	5 oz. (¼ pint)

OVEN TEMPERATURE EQUIVALENTS

Degrees Fahrenheit	Degrees Centigrade	Gas Mark No.	Example or Common Term
225°	107°	¼	Very Cool Oven
250°	121°	½	Very Cool Oven
275°	135°	1	Cool Oven
300°	149°	2	Cool Oven
325°	163°	3	Warm Oven
350°	177°	4	Moderate Oven
375°	191°	5	Fairly Hot
400°	204°	6	Hot
425°	218°	7	Hot
450°	232°	8	Very Hot
475°	246°	9	Very Hot
80-85°	26·7-29·4°		Yeast Dough Rises
98·6	37		Lukewarm (Body Temperature)
32°	0°		Water freezes
212°	100°		Water boils